CAMBRIDGE LIBRARY COLLECTION

Books of enduring scholarly value

Archaeology

The discovery of material remains from the recent or the ancient past has
always been a source of fascination, but the development of archaeology as
an academic discipline which interpreted such finds is relatively recent. It
was the work of Winckelmann at Pompeii in the 1760s which first revealed
the potential of systematic excavation to scholars and the wider public.
Pioneering figures of the nineteenth century such as Schliemann, Layard and
Petrie transformed archaeology from a search for ancient artifacts, by means
as crude as using gunpowder to break into a tomb, to a science which drew
from a wide range of disciplines - ancient languages and literature, geology,
chemistry, social history - to increase our understanding of human life and
society in the remote past.

An Account of Some Recent Discoveries in Hieroglyphical Literature and Egyptian Antiquities

Thomas Young (1773–1829) was an English physician who was one of the
first modern scholars to attempt to decipher ancient Egyptian hieroglyphs,
and made significant contributions to a variety of other academic disciplines.
He was elected a Fellow of the Royal Society in 1794 and in 1803 published
an article establishing the wave theory of light. Young became interested in
hieroglyphs in 1814, when he was sent a fragment of papyrus from Egypt.
After acquiring a copy of the Rosetta Stone inscriptions, Young made rapid
progress, publishing his results in 1816 and 1819. When Champollion
published his famous work on hieroglyphs in 1822, Young believed that this
had been based, without acknowledgement, on his own earlier translations,
which Champollion denied. This book was published in 1823 in an attempt
by Young to lay 'public claim to whatever credit be my due', and provides a
summary of his hieroglyphic research.

T0381581

Cambridge University Press has long been a pioneer in the reissuing of out-of-print titles from its own backlist, producing digital reprints of books that are still sought after by scholars and students but could not be reprinted economically using traditional technology. The Cambridge Library Collection extends this activity to a wider range of books which are still of importance to researchers and professionals, either for the source material they contain, or as landmarks in the history of their academic discipline.

Drawing from the world-renowned collections in the Cambridge University Library, and guided by the advice of experts in each subject area, Cambridge University Press is using state-of-the-art scanning machines in its own Printing House to capture the content of each book selected for inclusion. The files are processed to give a consistently clear, crisp image, and the books finished to the high quality standard for which the Press is recognised around the world. The latest print-on-demand technology ensures that the books will remain available indefinitely, and that orders for single or multiple copies can quickly be supplied.

The Cambridge Library Collection will bring back to life books of enduring scholarly value (including out-of-copyright works originally issued by other publishers) across a wide range of disciplines in the humanities and social sciences and in science and technology.

An Account of Some Recent Discoveries in Hieroglyphical Literature and Egyptian Antiquities

Including the Author's Original Alphabet, as Extended by Mr. Champollion, with a Translation of Five Unpublished Greek and Egyptian Manuscripts

THOMAS YOUNG

CAMBRIDGE
UNIVERSITY PRESS

CAMBRIDGE UNIVERSITY PRESS

Cambridge, New York, Melbourne, Madrid, Cape Town, Singapore,
São Paolo, Delhi, Dubai, Tokyo

Published in the United States of America by Cambridge University Press, New York

www.cambridge.org
Information on this title: www.cambridge.org/9781108017169

© in this compilation Cambridge University Press 2010

This edition first published 1823
This digitally printed version 2010

ISBN 978-1-108-01716-9 Paperback

AN ACCOUNT

OF

SOME RECENT DISCOVERIES

IN

HIEROGLYPHICAL LITERATURE,

AND

EGYPTIAN ANTIQUITIES.

INCLUDING

THE AUTHOR'S ORIGINAL ALPHABET,

AS EXTENDED BY MR. CHAMPOLLION,

WITH A

TRANSLATION OF FIVE UNPUBLISHED GREEK AND EGYPTIAN MANUSCRIPTS.

BY THOMAS YOUNG, M.D.F.R.S.

FELLOW OF THE ROYAL COLLEGE OF PHYSICIANS.

JOHN MURRAY, ALBEMARLE STREET.

1823.

TO ALEXANDER BARON VON HUMBOLDT,

AS A MARK OF THE HIGHEST RESPECT,

FOR THE EXTENT OF HIS KNOWLEDGE

AND THE ACCURACY OF HIS RESEARCH,

AS WELL AS

FOR HIS ARDENT ZEAL IN THE PROMOTION OF SCIENCE,

AND FOR HIS CANDOUR AND VIGILANCE

IN THE DISTRIBUTION OF LITERARY JUSTICE,

THIS WORK IS DEDICATED

BY HIS OBLIGED FRIEND,

THE AUTHOR.

VOLVENDA DIES EN ATTULIT ULTRO!

CONTENTS.

PREFACE.

A COMPLETE confirmation of the principal results, which I had some years since deduced, from an examination of the hieroglyphical monuments of ancient Egypt, having been very unexpectedly derived from the ulterior researches of Mr. Champollion, and from the singular good fortune of Mr. George Grey, I cannot resist the natural inclination, to make a public claim to whatever credit may be my due, for the labour that I have bestowed, on an attempt to unveil the mystery, in which Egyptian literature has been involved for nearly twenty centuries.

If, indeed, I have not hitherto wholly withheld from the public the results of my inquiries, it has not been from the love of

authorship only, nor from an impatience of
being the sole possessor of a secret treasure ;
but because I was desirous of securing, at
least, for my country, what is justly considered as a desirable acquisition to every
country, the reputation of having enlarged
the boundaries of human knowledge, and of
having contributed to extend the dominion
of the mind of man over time, and space,
and neglect, and obscurity. *Corona in*
SACRIS CERTAMINIBUS *non victori datur,*
sed PATRIA *ab eo coronari pronuntiatur.* And
whatever vanity or enthusiasm there might be
in this sentiment, it was at least sincere and
unaffected.

In the mean time my Egyptian investigations had been as laborious as they had
been persevering : and like many other
pursuits, in which I have been engaged, they
had been so little enlivened by any fortunate
coincidences, or unexpected facilities, that
having occasion to adopt a motto for the sig-

natures of some anonymous communications, I had chosen the words FORTUNAM EX ALIIS, as appropriate to my own history. But the new lights, which Mr. Champollion has obtained, and the marvellous accident of the existence of a Greek manuscript, in perfect preservation, which I found, when Mr. Grey had obligingly left it for my examination, to be the translation of a unique hieroglyphic papyrus, lately purchased by the King of France; these circumstances have so far changed the complexion of my literary adventures, that if I remained any longer in masquerade, I should certainly be compelled to adopt the character of POLYCRATES or of ALADDIN.

It would indeed have been a little hard, that the only single step, which leads at once to an extensive result, should have been made by a Foreigner, upon the very ground which I had undergone the drudgery of quietly raising, while he advanced rapidly

and firmly, without denying his obligations
to his predecessor, but very naturally, under
all circumstances, without exaggerating them,
or indeed very fully enumerating them. I
should not have repined, even if no counter-
part to his good fortune had occurred for my
own advantage and assistance; but the exhi-
laration of a success, so unexpected, has
brought me more immediately and more
openly before the public, than it was pre-
viously my intention to appear, in relation
to a pursuit so remote from the nature of
many other duties which I am bound to fulfil.

It may naturally be expected that I should
make some apology, for what is generally
considered as a violation of professional
decorum; for presuming to appear again
before the public, without absolute neces-
sity, in any other capacity than that of a
practical physician. I have indeed myself
observed, on a former occasion, that the
public is inclined to think, and not with-

out something like reason, that the abilities of different individuals are pretty nearly equal; and that if any one has distinguished himself in a particular department of study, he must have bestowed so much the less time and attention on other departments: that, of course, if he excelled in more than one line, out of his profession, the natural inference would be so much the stronger: and that whether this may be fair or not, it is at least fair, that direct evidence should be produced or imagined of a devotion to medical pursuits, before medical confidence can reasonably be expected.

My explanation then is, that I consider myself as having already produced to the public *more than sufficient* " evidence" of my claim to this " medical confidence"; and that, having now acquired the right to celebrate a YEAR of JUBILEE, I think myself fully justified in endeavouring, without further regard to the strict etiquette of my profession, to obtain, while I have yet a few

years more to live and to learn, whatever
respect may be thought due to the discoveries,
which have constituted the amusement of a
few of my leisure hours.

In addition to this apology, perhaps already
too long, I will venture to state, as a matter
of anecdote, the train of occurrences that has
accidentally led me to engage in these pursuits. To begin therefore with the beginning,
or rather before the beginning, as the subject
of a preface may very naturally do: I had
been induced by motives both of private
friendship, and of professional obligation, to
offer, to the editors of a periodical publication,
an article, which I thought would be of some
advantage to their collection, containing an
abstract of Adelung's Mithridates, a work
then lately received from the continent. In
reading this elaborate compilation, my curiosity was excited by a note of the editor,
Professor Vater, in which he asserted that
the unknown language of the Stone of

Rosetta, and of the bandages often found with the mummies, was capable of being analysed into an alphabet consisting of little more than thirty letters : but having merely retained this general impression, I thought no more of these inscriptions, until they were recalled to my attention, by the examination of some fragments of a papyrus, which had been brought home from Egypt by my friend Sir William Rouse Boughton, then lately returned from his travels in the East. With this accidental occurrence my Egyptian researches began : their progress and termination will be the subject of the present volume.

T. Y.

Welbeck Street,
1 *March,* 1823.

WORKS OF THE AUTHOR;

TO BE HAD OF THE PUBLISHER.

1. A Course of Lectures on Natural Philosophy and the Mechanical Arts, 2 vols. 4to. 1807.

2. An Introduction to Medical Literature, including a System of Practical Nosology, 8vo. Second edition, 1823.

3. A Practical and Historical Treatise on Consumptive Diseases, 8vo. 1815.

4. Elementary Illustrations of the Celestial Mechanics of Laplace, 8vo. 1821.

DISCOVERIES

IN

HIEROGLYPHICAL LITERATURE.

————

CHAPTER I.

INTRODUCTORY SKETCH OF THE PREVALENT OPI-
NIONS RESPECTING HIEROGLYPHICS.

THE Greeks and Romans, either from national
pride, or from a want of philological talent, were
extremely deficient in their knowledge of all such
languages as they called barbarous, and they frequently made up for their ignorance by the posi-
tiveness of their assertions, with regard to facts
which were created by their own imagination. It
was very currently believed, on their authority, not
only that Egypt was the parent of all arts and sciences, but that the hieroglyphical inscriptions, on its
public monuments, contained a summary of the
most important mysteries of nature, and of the
most sublime inventions of man: but that the interpretation of these characters had been so stu-
diously concealed by the priests, from the knowledge of the vulgar, and had indeed been so im-

perfectly understood by themselves, that it was
wholly lost and forgotten in the days of the later
Roman Emperors. The story, however, of a re-
ward, supposed to have been offered in vain by
one of the first of the Caesars, for an interpretation
of the inscription on an obelisc, then lately brought
from Egypt to Rome, appears to rest on no au-
thentic foundation.

Among the works of more modern authors, who
had employed themselves in the study of the hieroglyphics, it is difficult to say whether those were the
more discouraging, which, like the productions of
Father Kircher and the Chevalier Palin, professed
to contain explanations of every thing, or which,
like the ponderous volume of Zoëga on the Obeliscs, confessed, after collecting all that was really
on record, that the sum and substance of the
whole amounted absolutely to nothing.

Father Kircher's six folios contain some tole-
rably faithful, though inelegant, representations of
the principal monuments of Egyptian art, which
had before his days been brought to Europe: and,
according to his interpretation, which succeeded
equally well, whether he happened to begin at
the beginning, or at the end, of each of the lines,
they all contain some mysterious doctrines of religion or of metaphysics. With equal sagacity, but
with much less appearance of laborious research,
the Chevalier Palin, beginning, in one instance at
least, by way of variety, in the middle, has more

recently discovered, that Hebrew translations of
many of the Egyptian consecrated rolls of papyrus
are to be found, in the Bible, under the name of
the Psalms of David. Whatever may be thought
of the judgment of these antiquaries, their opinions are not particularly discreditable to their
talents and ingenuity: for having once allowed
themselves to set out with the mistaken notion,
that it was possible to determine the sense of
the hieroglyphics, by internal evidence and by the
force of reasoning only, the imperfections of their
superstructures were the unavoidable consequences of the unsubstantial nature of the foundations, on which they were raised.

There was indeed a traditional record of the
true sense of one single character, denoting LIFE,
which had been handed down by the ecclesias-
tical writers, and had been generally received as
correct by scholars and antiquaries : although I
cannot help suspecting that Sir Archibald Ed-
monstone's memory deceives him when he remarks, that the same symbol is often substituted,
in Christian inscriptions, for the simpler sign of
the cross, with which they more commonly begin.
We also find some imperfect hints of a partial
knowledge of the sense of the hieroglyphics in
the puerile work of Horapollo, which is much
more like a collection of conceits and enigmas
than an explanation of a real system of serious
literature : and while such scattered truths were

confounded with a multitude of false assertions, it was impossible to profit by any of them, without some clue to assist us in the selection. For my own part, if I had ever read of the true signification of the handled cross, it had entirely escaped my recollection.

The French expedition to Egypt was most liberally provided, by the government of the day, with a select body of antiquaries, and architects, and surveyors, and naturalists, and draughtsmen, whose business it was to investigate all that was interesting to science or to literature in that singular country. Their labours have been made public, with all the advantages of chalcographical and typographical elegance, in the splendid collection, entitled *Déscription de l'Egypte*. But it is scarcely too much to say, that the only real benefit, conferred on Egyptian literature, by that expedition, was the discovery of a huge broken block, of black stone, in digging for the foundations of Fort St. Julian, near Rosetta, which the British army had afterwards the honour of bringing to this country, as a proud trophy of their gallantry and success. It is not to a want of ability, nor of industry, nor of accuracy, nor of fidelity, in the Egyptian Commission, that so total a failure is to be attributed; but partly to the real difficulty of the subject, and still more to the preconceived opinion, which was very generally entertained by their men of letters, of the exorbitant antiquity of the Egyptian works of art, which caused them to neglect the lights, that might have been derived, from a comparison of Greek and Roman inscriptions, with the hieroglyphics in their neighbourhood; and to suppose, that whatever bore the date of less than thirty or forty centuries must necessarily be an interpolation, unconnected with the original architecture and decorations of the edifice, to which it belonged: and when a strong prejudice has once been imbibed, we all know that the senses themselves are perpetually blunted and perverted by it, even without the consent of the reasoning powers. Mr. William Hamilton had, however, very successfully brought forwards a variety of evidence, in favour of the utility of the various inscriptions of the Greeks and Romans, for ascertaining the date of many of the buildings to which they belong; and the question, thus agitated between the French and the English travellers, had already assumed somewhat of a national character.

A cursory inspection of the Greek inscription, contained in the pillar of Rosetta, was sufficient to establish, as incontrovertible, the opinion, which had been very ably maintained by our acute and learned countryman Bishop Warburton, that the hieroglyphics, or sacred characters, were not so denominated, as being exclusively appropriated to sacred subjects, but that they constituted a real written language, applicable to the purposes of history and common life, as well as to those of religion and mythology; since this inscription speaks of the three divisions of the pillar, as containing different versions of the same decree, in the sacred and the vulgar character, and in the Greek language, respectively: and, that there was no fraud in this description, was at once made evident by the just observation of Akerblad, who pointed out, at the end of the hieroglyphical inscription, the three first numerals, indicated by I, II, and III, respectively, where the Greek has "the first and the second ..."; the end being broken off. It was also evident, that the hieroglyphical language continued to be understood and employed in the time of Ptolemy Epiphanes: but he₁e the matter rested for several years; no single representation of an existing object having been so identified, on this or any other monument among the hieroglyphics, as to have its signification determined, even by a probable conjecture.

In the mean time, the enterprising and enlightened Baron Alexander Von Humboldt was contributing to illustrate the nature of hieroglyphical languages, by his account of the Mexican drawings, contained in his Views of the Cordilleras and Monuments of the American nations. The symbols, however, of the Americans appear to have had little or nothing in common with those of the Egyptians. The written language of the Chinese, on the contrary, exhibits, in some cases, a much closer analogy with that of ancient Egypt: and Mr. Barrow, by his clear and concise explanation of the peculiar nature of the Chinese characters, has contributed very materially to assist us in tracing the gradual progress of the Egyptian symbols through their various forms; although the resemblance is certainly far less complete than has been supposed by Mr. Palin, who tells us, that we have only to translate the Psalms of David into Chinese, and to write them in the ancient character of that language, in order to reproduce the Egyptian papyri, that are found with the mummies.

CHAPTER II.

THE pillar of Rosetta was now safely and quietly deposited in the British Museum; the Society of Antiquaries had engraved, and very generally circulated, a correct copy of its three inscriptions; and several of the best scholars of the age, in particular Porson and Heyne, had employed themselves in completing and illustrating the Greek text, which constituted the third part of the inscription: and it so happened that, although no person acquainted with both these critics could hesitate to give the general preference, for acuteness of observation, and felicity of conjecture, and soundness of judgment, to the English professor, yet in this instance the superior industry and vigilance of the German had given him decidedly the advantage, with respect to two or three passages, in which their translations happen to differ.

But Greek was already sufficiently understood, both in London and at Gottingen, to make this part of the investigation comparatively insignificant. Mr. Akerblad, a diplomatic gentleman, then at Paris, but afterwards the Swedish resident at Rome, had begun to decipher the middle division of the inscription; after De Sacy had given up the pursuit as hopeless, notwithstanding that he had made out very satisfactorily the names of Ptolemy and Alexander. But both he and Mr. Akerblad proceeded upon the erroneous, or, at least imperfect, evidence of the Greek authors, who have pretended to explain the different modes of writing among the ancient Egyptians, and who have asserted very distinctly that they employed, on many occasions, an alphabetical system, composed of twenty five letters only. The characters of the second part of the inscription being called in the Greek ENCHORIA GRAMMATA, or letters of the country, it was natural to look among these for the alphabet in question: and Mr. Akerblad, having principally deduced his conclusions from the preamble of the decree, which consists in great measure of foreign proper names, persisted, to the time of his death, in believing, that this part of the inscription was throughout alphabetical. I have called these characters enchoric, or rather *enchorial:* Mr. Champollion has chosen to distinguish them by the term *demotic,* or popular; perhaps from having been in the habit of employing it before he was acquainted with the denomination which I had appropriated to them: in my opinion, the priority of my publication ought to have induced him to adopt my term, and to suppress his own, rather than to add another useless synonym, for what the ancients, when speaking with accuracy, would probably have described as the " epistolographic" form of writing employed by the Egyptians: for we have no means of determining the precise nature of the characters called *popular* by Herodotus.

Mr. Akerblad was far from having completed his examination of the whole enchorial inscription, apparently from the want of some collateral encouragement or cooperation, to induce him to continue so laborious an inquiry; and he had made little or no effort to understand the first inscription of the pillar, which is professedly engraved in the sacred character, except the detached observation, respecting the numerals at the end: he was even disposed to acquiesce in the correctness of Mr. Palin's interpretation, which proceeds on the supposition, that parts of the first lines of the hieroglyphics are still remaining on the stone.

It was natural to expect, that, after the possibility of a partial success, in this part of the undertaking, had been almost demonstrated by what Mr. Akerblad had cursorily observed, the critics and chronologists of all civilised countries would have united, heart and hand, in a common effort to obtain a legitimate solution of all the doubts and difficulties, in which the early antiquities of Egypt had long remained involved. But, excepting Mr. Champollion and myself, they have all chosen to amuse themselves with their own speculations and conjectures: the mathematicians of France have continued to calculate, and the metaphysicians of England have continued to argue, upon elements which it was impossible either to prove or disprove; while the fortuitous coincidences of some accidental results, with the collateral testimony of history or of astronomy, have been forced into the service of the delusion, as evidences of the truth of the hypotheses from which they had been deduced. Nor are these amusements even at this moment discontinued, by some persons, who have shown themselves capable of doing better things.

It was early in the year 1814, that I had been examining the fragments of papyrus brought from Egypt by Mr. Boughton; and that, after looking over Mr. Akerblad's pamphlet in a hasty manner, I communicated a few anonymous remarks on them to the Society of Antiquaries. In the summer of that year, I took the triple inscription with me to Worthing, and there proceeded to examine first the enchorial inscription, and afterwards the sacred characters. By an attentive and methodical comparison of the different parts with each other, I had sufficiently deciphered the whole, in the course of a few months, to be able to send, as an appendix to the paper printed in the Archaeologia, a translation of each of the Egyptian inscriptions considered separately, distinguishing the contents of the different lines, with as much precision as my ma-

terials would enable me to obtain. It is evident
that this division of the translation supposes, in
general, a distinction of the significations of the
single words; and that any person, with a little
attention, might retrace my steps, with regard to
the sense that I attributed to each part of the two
inscriptions. I was obliged to leave many important passages still subject to some doubt, and
I hoped to acquire additional information, before
I attempted to determine their signification with
accuracy; but, having made the first great step,
I concluded that many others might be added
with facility and with rapidity In this conclusion,
however, I was somewhat mistaken; and when
we reflect that, in the case of the Chinese, the
only hieroglyphical language now extant, it is
considered as a task requiring the whole labour
of a learned life, to become acquainted with the
greater part of the words, even among those who
are in the habit of employing the same language
for the ordinary purposes of life, and who have
the assistance of accurate and voluminous gram-
mars and dictionaries: we shall then be at no
loss to understand that a hieroglyphical language,
to be acquired by means of the precarious aid of
a few monuments, which have accidentally escaped
the ravages of time and of barbarism, must exhibit
a combination of difficulties almost insurmountable to human industry.

I had thought it necessary, in the pursuit of
the inquiry, to make myself in some measure

familiar with the remains of the old Egyptian language, as they are preserved in the Coptic and Thebaic versions of the Scriptures; and I had hoped, with the assistance of this knowledge, to be able to find an alphabet, which would enable me to read the enchorial inscription at least into a kindred dialect. But, in the progress of the investigation, I had gradually been compelled to abandon this expectation, and to admit the conviction, that no such alphabet would ever be discovered, because it had never been in existence.

I was led to this conclusion, not only by the untractable nature of the inscription itself, which might have depended on my own want of information or of address, but still more decidedly by the manifest occurrence of a multitude of characters, which were obviously imperfect imitations of the more intelligible pictures, that were observable among the distinct hieroglyphics of the first inscription: such as a Priest, a Statue, and a Mattock or Plough, which were evidently, in their primitive state, delineations of the objects intended to be denoted by them, and which were as evidently introduced among the enchorial characters. But whether or no any other significant words were expressed, in the same inscription, by means of the alphabet employed in it for foreign names, I could not very satisfactorily determine.

A cursory examination of the few well identified characters, amounting to about 90 or 100, which the hieroglyphical inscription, in its mutilated state, had enabled me to ascertain, was however sufficient to prove, first, that many simple objects were represented, as might naturally be supposed, by their actual delineations; secondly, that many other objects, represented graphically, were used in a figurative sense only, while a great number of the symbols, in frequent use, could be considered as the pictures of no existing objects whatever; thirdly, that, in order to express a plurality of objects, a dual was denoted by a repetition of the character, but that three characters of the same kind, following each other, implied an indefinite plurality, which was likewise more compendiously represented by means of three lines or bars attached to a single character; fourthly, that definite numbers were expressed by dashes for units, and arches, either round or square, for tens; fifthly, that all hieroglyphical inscriptions were read from front to rear, as the objects naturally follow each other; sixthly, that proper names were included by the oval ring, or border, or *cartouche*, of the sacred characters, and often between two fragments of a similar border in the running hand; and, seventhly, that the name of Ptolemy alone existed on this pillar, having only been completely identified by the assistance of the analysis of the enchorial inscription.   And, as far as I have ever heard or read, *not one* of these particulars had ever been established and placed on record, by *any other* person, dead or alive.

CHAPTER III.

MY full conviction respecting the nature and origin of the enchorial character I expressed at the end of a collection of letters, inserted in the MUSEUM CRITICUM, and published in 1815. It was not, however, till the next year, that I obtained the most complete evidence of the truth of my opinion: having been obligingly accommodated, by Mr. William Hamilton, with the use of his copy of the great *Description de l'Egypte*, as far as it was then published, I proceeded to study its contents: and I discovered, at length, that several of the manuscripts on papyrus, which had been carefully published in that work, exhibited very frequently the same text in different forms, deviating more or less from the perfect resemblance of the objects intended to be delineated, till they became, in many cases, mere lines and curves, and dashes and flourishes; but still answering, character for character, to the hieroglyphical or hieratic writing of the same chapters, found in other manuscripts, and of which the identity was sufficiently indicated, besides this coincidence, by the similarity of the larger tablets, or pictural representations, at the head of each chapter or column, which are almost universally found on the margins of manuscripts of a mythological nature. And the enchorial inscription of the pillar of Rosetta resembled very accurately, in its general appearance, the most unpicturesque of these manuscripts. It did not, however, by any means agree, character for character, with the "sacred letters" of the first inscription, though in many instances, by means of some intermediate steps derived from the manuscripts on papyrus, the characters could be traced into each other with sufficient accuracy, to supersede every idea of any essential diversity in the principles of representation employed. The want of a more perfect correspondence could only be explained, by considering the sacred characters as the remains of a more ancient and solemn mode of expression, which had been superseded, in common life, by other words and phrases; and, in several cases, it seemed probable. that the forms of the characters had been so far degraded and confused, that the addition of a greater number of distinguishing epithets had become necessary, in order that the sense might be rendered intelligible.

A particular account of this comparison of the different modes of writing, and a detailed reference to the passages of the respective manuscripts from which they were derived, is contained in two letters, printed in 1816, as a part of the seventh number of the Museum Criticum, and of which several copies were immediately sent to Paris, and to other parts of the Continent, although the actual publication of the number was retarded till 1821.

The principal contents of these letters were, however, incorporated with other matter into a more extensive article, which I contributed in 1819 to the Supplement of the Encyclopaedia Britannica. I had made drawings of the plates, which were engraved with great fidelity by Mr. Turrell, about a year before; and having been favoured by the proprietors with a few separate copies, I had sent them to some of my friends, in the summer of 1818, with a cover, on which was printed the title Hieroglyphical Vocabulary: these plates, however, were precisely the same that were afterwards contained in the fourth volume of the Supplement, as belonging to the article Egypt.

The characters explained, with confidence, in this vocabulary, amounted to about 200; the number which had been immediately obtained from the pillar of Rosetta having been somewhat more than doubled by means of a careful examination of other monuments, on which the terms god, and king, and other epithets, already ascertained, were so applied as to furnish either certain or probable conclusions respecting the principal deities of the Egyptians, and respecting several of the latest and the most celebrated of their sovereigns. The higher numerals were readily obtained, by a comparison of some inscriptions, in which they stood combined with units and with tens. The hieratic manuscripts assisted also in this identification, by facilitating the determination of the hieroglyphic corresponding to a given enchorial character. The names of Phthah and of Apis were still left on the pillar: to these I was now enabled to add, with tolerable certainty, those of Ammon, or Jupiter, Phre, or the Sun, Rhea, or Urania, Ioh, or the Moon, Thoth, or Hermes, Osiris, Arueris, or Apollo, Isis, Nephthe, Buto, Horus, and Mneuis; besides a multitude of others, to whom I found it convenient to appropriate fictitious or temporary appellations, for the greater convenience of reference. Thus I have called Cerexochus, a figure whose real name was perhaps Amonrasonther, and my Hyperion and Platypterus are supposed by Mr. Champollion to belong to Horus and to Hercules. Of the kings, I have ascertained, as far as the testimony of the Greek and Latin historians and inscriptions would enable me, the names of Mesphres, Memnon, Sesostris, Nechao, Psammis, and Amasis; and having obtained the distinction of Ptolemy Soter from the pillar, I afterwards determined, by its assistance, the name of his queen Berenice. The termination indicating the female sex was another important result of this comparison of various monuments.

I must acknowledge that my respect for the good sense and accomplishments of my Egyptian allies by no means became more profound as our acquaintance became more intimate: on the contrary, all that Juvenal, in a moment, as might have been supposed, of discontent, had held up to ridicule of their superstitions and their depravity, became, as it were, displayed before my eyes, as the details of their mythology became more intelligible. That Plato professed to have learned much during a long residence in Egypt I can easily believe: he may very probably have derived from thence some hints, that led to his own purer doctrines of the immortality of the soul, although he may have been tempted to exaggerate a little the other advantages of his travels in search of truth; but that Pythagoras ever professed to have acquired any solid knowledge from the Egyptians, appears to me to be very inconsistent with what we know of the history of this illustrious philosopher, speculative and visionary as some of his arithmetical metaphysics seem to have been. I shall enter into some further details of my conclusions, in the words which I have already employed in the article EGYPT.

" By means of the knowledge of the hieroglyphical characters, which has been already obtained,
we are fully competent to form a general idea of
the nature· of the inscriptions on the principal
Egyptian monuments that are extant. Numerous
as they are, there is scarcely one of them which
we are not able to refer to the class either of
sepulchral or of votive inscriptions; astronomical
and chronological there seem to be none, since
the numerical characters, which have been perfectly ascertained, have not yet been found to
occur in such a form as they necessarily must
have assumed in the records of this description:
of a historical nature, we can only find the triumphal, which are often sufficiently distinguishable, but they may also always be referred to the
votive; since whoever related his own exploits
thought it wisest to attribute the glory of them to
some deity, and whoever recorded those of another was generally disposed to intermix divine
honours with his panegyric.   It has, indeed, been
asserted, that the Egyptians were not in the habit
of deifying any mortal persons; but the inscription of Rosetta is by no means the only one in
which the sovereigns of Egypt are inserted in the
number of its deities; the custom is observable
in monuments of a much earlier age: indeed, in
such a country, it might be considered as a kind
of dilemma of degradation, whether it was most
ridiculous to be made a divinity, or to be ex-

cluded from so plebeian an assemblage; but flattery is more prone to err by commission than by omission, and, consequently, we find the terms king and god very generally inseparable. The sepulchral inscriptions, from the attention that was paid in Egypt to the obsequies of the dead, appear, on the whole, to constitute the most considerable part of the Egyptian literature which remains, and they afford us, upon a comparative examination, some very remarkable peculiarities. The general tenor of all these inscriptions appears to be, as might be expected from the testimony of Herodotus, the identification of the deceased with the god Osiris, and probably, if a female, with Isis; and the subject of the most usual representations seems to be the reception of this new personage by the principal deities, to whom he now stands in a relation expressed in the respective inscriptions; the honour of an apotheosis, reserved by the ancient Romans for emperors, and by the modern for saints, having been apparently extended by the old Egyptians to private individuals of all descriptions [; as indeed appears to be partially hinted in the concluding line of the golden verses of the Pythagoreans] It required an extensive comparison of these inscriptions to recognise their precise nature, since they seldom contain a name surrounded by a ring in its usual form: sometimes, however, as in the green sarcophagus of the British Museum, a dis-

tinct name is very often repeated, and preceded
by that of Osiris; while, in most other instances,
there is a certain combination of characters, bearing evident relation to the personage delineated,
which occurs, after the symbols of Osiris, instead
of the name; so that either the ring was simply
omitted on this occasion, or a new and perhaps
a mysterious name was employed, consisting frequently of the appellations of several distinct
deities, and probably analogous to the real name[,
which will, indeed, hereafter appear to have con-
sisted not uncommonly of a similar combination].
That the characteristic phrase [,or group], so repeated, must have had some relation to the deceased, is proved by its scarcely ever being alike
in any two monuments that have been compared,
while almost every other part of the manuscripts
and inscriptions are the same in many different
instances, and some of them in almost all; and
this same phrase may be observed in Lord Mountnorris's and Mr. Bankes's manuscripts, placed
over the head of the person who is brought up
between the two goddesses, to make his appearance before the true Osiris, in his own person, and
in his judicial capacity, with his counsellors about
him, and the balance of justice before him." . . .

" The tablet of the last judgment, which is so
well illustrated by the testimony of Diodorus
concerning the funerals of the Egyptians, is found
near the end of almost all the manuscripts upon

papyrus, that are so frequently discovered in the coffins of the mummies, and among others in Lord Mountnorris's hieratic manuscript, printed in the collection of the Egyptian Society. The great deity sits on the left, holding the hook and the whip or fan; his name and titles are generally placed over him; but this part of the present manuscript is a little injured. Before him is a kind of mace, supporting something like the skin of a leopard; then a female Cerberus, and on a shelf over her head, the tetrad of termini, which have been already distinguished by the names " Tetrarcha," Anubis, Macedo, and " Hieracion," each having had his appropriate denomination written over his head. Behind the Cerberis stands Thoth, with his style and tablet, having just begun to write. Over his head, in two columns, we find his name and titles, including his designation as a scribe. The balance follows, with a little baboon as a kind of genius, sitting on it. Under the beam stand " Cteristes" and " Hyperion" [supposed by Mr. Champollion to be Anubis and Horus], who are employed in adjusting the equipoise; but their names in this manuscript are omitted. The five columns over the balance are only remarkable as containing, in this instance, the characteristic phrase, or the name of the deceased, intermixed with other characters. Beyond the balance stands a female, holding the sceptre of Isis, who seems to be called

Rhea, the wife of the Sun. She is looking back
at the personage, who holds up his hand as a mark
of respect, and who is identified as the deceased
by the name simply placed over him, without any
exordium. ·He is followed by a second goddess,
who is also holding up her hands, in token of
respect; and whose name looks like a personifi-
cation of honour or glory, unless it is simply intended to signify "a divine priestess," belonging
to the order of the Pterophori, mentioned on the
Rosetta stone. The forty two assessors, [no-
ticed by Diodorus and by these manuscripts],
are wanting in this tablet; and, in many other
manuscripts their number is curtailed, to make
room for other subjects; but, in several of those
which are engraved in the *Déscription de l'Egypte*,
they are all represented, sometimes as sitting
figures, and sometimes standing as termini, with
their feet united."

"The principal part of the text of all these
manuscripts appears to consist of a collection of
hymns, or rather homages, to certain deities, generally expressed in the name of the deceased,
with his title of Osiris, although the true Osiris
is not excluded from the groups that are introduced. The upper part of each manuscript is
occupied by a series of pictural tablets; under
them are vertical columns of distinct hieroglyphics, or, in the epistolographic manuscripts,
pages of the text, which are commonly divided

into paragraphs, with a tablet at the head of each;
the first words being constantly written with red
ink, made of a kind of ochre, as the black is of a
carbonaceous substance. The beginning of the
manuscripts is seldom entire, being always at the
outside of the roll; as the *umbilicus* of the
Romans was synonymous with the end." . .

" The coffins of the mummies, and the larger
sarcophagi of stone, are generally covered with
representations extremely similar to some of
those which are found in the manuscripts. The
judicial tablet is frequently delineated on the
middle of the coffins; above it are Isis and
Nephthe, at the sides, and apparently Rhea in
the middle, with outspread wings. The space
below is chiefly occupied by figures of twenty or
thirty of the principal deities, to whom the deceased, in his mystical character, is doing
homage; each of them being probably designated
by the relationship in which he stands to the new
representative of Osiris. In the sculptures, the
figures are generally less numerous; the same
deities are commonly represented as on the
painted coffins, but without the repetition of the
suppliant, and in an order subject to some little
variation. The large sarcophagus of granite, in
the British Museum, brought from Cairo, and
formerly called the Lover's Fountain, has the
name of Apis, as a part of the characteristic denomination. This circumstance, at first sight,

seemed to make it evident that it must have been
intended to contain the mummy of an Apis, for
which its magnitude renders it well calculated ;
but when the symbols of other deities were found
in the mystic names upon various other monuments, this inference could no longer be considered as absolutely conclusive." . .

" Of the triumphal monuments, the most magnificent are the obeliscs, which are reported by
Pliny to have been dedicated to the Sun; and
there is every reason to suppose, that the translation of one of these inscriptions, preserved by Am-
mianus Marcellinus, after Hermapion, contains a
true representation of a part of its contents, more
especially as ' the mighty Apollo' of Hermapion
agrees completely with the hawk, the bull, and
the arm, which usually occupy the beginning of
each inscription. These symbols are generally
followed by a number of pompous titles, not always very intimately connected with each other,
and among them we often find that of ' Lord of
the asp bearing diadems,' with some others, immediately preceding the name and parentage of
the sovereign, who is the principal subject of the
inscription. The obelisc at Heliopolis is without
the bull; and the whole inscription may be supposed to have signified something of this kind.

" THIS APOLLINEAN TROPHY IS CONSECRATED
TO THE HONOUR OF KING ' REMESSES,' CROWNED

WITH AN ASP BEARING DIADEM; IT IS CONSE-
CRATED TO THE HONOUR OF THE SON OF 'HERON,'
THE ORNAMENT OF HIS COUNTRY, BELOVED BY
PHTHAH, LIVING FOR EVER; IT IS CONSECRATED
TO THE HONOUR OF THE REVERED AND BENEFICIENT
DEITY 'REMESSES,' GREAT IN GLORY, SUPERIOR TO
HIS ENEMIES; BY THE DECREE OF AN ASSEMBLY,
TO THE POWERFUL AND THE FLOURISHING, WHOSE
LIFE SHALL BE WITHOUT END."

"It is true, that some parts of this interpretation
are in great measure conjectural; but none of it
is altogether arbitrary, or unsupported by some
probable analogy: and the spirit and tenor of the
inscription is probably unimpaired by the altera-
tions, which this approximation to the sense may
unavoidably have introduced.

"Of the obeliscs, still in existence, there are
perhaps about thirty, larger and smaller, which
may be considered as genuine. Several others
are decidedly spurious, having been chiefly sculptured at Rome, in imitation of the Egyptian style,
but so negligently and unskilfully, as to have exhibited a striking difference even in the character of
the workmanship. Such are the Pamphilian, in
explanation of which the laborious Kircher has
published a folio volume, and the Barberinian
or Veranian: in both of these the emblems are
put together in a manner wholly arbitrary; and
when an attempt is made to imitate the appear-

ance of a name, the characters are completely
different at each repetition   The Sallustian obelisc has also been broken, and joined inaccurately,
and some modern restitutions have been very
awkwardly introduced, as becomes evident upon
comparing with each other the figures of Kircher
and of Zoëga. [A similar restitution has been
rather better executed at one corner of the La-
teran obelisc, as I observed in the course of a few
weeks that I passed at Rome in the summer of
1821: the block of granite, which has been employed, still exhibits some words of a Latin
inscription, turned upside down, but not effaced,
although the hieroglyphics belonging to the
place have been imitated with tolerable fidelity].
Another very celebrated monument, the Isiac
table, which has been the subject of much profound discussion, and has given birth to many
refined mythological speculations, is equally in-
capable of supporting a minute examination upon
solid grounds; for the inscriptions neither bear
any relation to the figures near which they are
placed, nor form any connected sense of their
own; and the whole is undoubtedly the work of
a Roman sculptor, imitating only the general
style and the separate delineations of the Egyptian tablets; as indeed some of the most learned
and acute of our critical antiquaries had already
asserted, notwithstanding the contrary opinion of
several foreigners, of the highest reputation for

their intimate acquaintance with the works of Greek and Roman art. We may hope, however, that in future these unprofitable discussions and disputes will become less and less frequent, and that our knowledge of the antiquities of Egypt will gain as much in the solidity and sufficiency of its inedence, as it may probably lose in its hyothetical symmetry and its imaginary extent; and while we allow every latitude to legitimate reasoning and cautious conjecture, in the search after historical truths, we must peremptorily exclude from our investigations an attachment to fanciful systems and presupposed analogies on the one hand, and a too implicit deference to traditional authority on the other."

A few general remarks, that I had taken the liberty of sending out to Mr. William Bankes, for his assistance in his Egyptian researches, had been found of some utility in directing his attention to points of the most material importance for the promotion of the investigation: and even before the actual publication of the Supplement of the Encyclopaedia, I had received from Egypt a very agreeable confirmation of my opinions, in a letter addressed by Mr. Salt to Mr. William Hamilton, of which I shall here insert an extract.

" Cairo, 1st May, 1819.

" At Dakki in Nubia there is an inscription of the Ptolemies, over the principal entrance, that

occupies a place evidently connected with the
architecture; and on each side of this is a tablet of
hieroglyphics, nearly similar one to the other. Now
it struck me on the spot, that these, being nearly of
the same length as the Greek tablet, might possibly
contain a translation. I therefore referred to a letter
in Mr. Bankes's possession, containing some fifty
explanations of hieroglyphics from Dr. Young,
and was certainly gratified to find that in the oval
[ring], conspicuous on each side, was the name of
the "immortal Ptolemy": and immediately afterwards the name of Hermes on one side, and of
Isis on the other, to whom, by numerous Greek
inscriptions, it is certain that the temple was dedicated. In following up this idea, I found, in
other parts of the temple, the name of "Ptolemy"
without the "immortal," over offering figures;
and also those hieroglyphics which Dr. Young supposes to represent the names of Osiris, Isis, and
Horus, as well as Hermes, over their respective
figures, invariably, I may say, throughout the
numerous representations on the walls. . .

H. S."

Upon Mr. Bankes's return to England, he had
the kindness and liberality to allow me free access
to the unequalled treasures of drawings and inscriptions, that he had accumulated and brought
home; and I soon obtained a knowledge of several
additional characters from the comparison of these
valuable documents. The most useful of these was

the symbol for BROTHER or SISTER, which appears
to be the crook generally seen in the hands of Osiris,
and which is closely imitated in the enchorial character that I had already ascertained. I found, also,
that the emblem which I had taken for MOTHER
could only be translated WIFE, as it was applied to
Cleopatra with relation to her husband Ptolemy;
and that a FATHER was denoted by a bird with
an arm, as I had at first inferred from the pillar of
Rosetta, though I afterwards abandoned the opinion, from supposing that I had found another
emblem for Ptolemy Philopator. It happened,
however, by mere accident, that the advantage
which I derived from this source was much less
considerable than might have been expected,
both from its abundance and from its unconta-
minated purity; but I had been rather disposed
to defer the ultimate study of Mr. Bankes's collections, till their publication should give me a
free right to employ them in any manner that I
might think proper. Some remarks, however,
that occurred to me in consequence of looking
them over, I incorporated in a little essay which
I gave to Mr. Belzoni, and which makes the appendix to the second edition of his travels. I
have here observed, in speaking of the reference
of the supposed Jewish captives, exhibited in the
catacomb of my " Psammis," to the expeditions of
Necho to Jerusalem, in the time of King Josiah
and Jehoahaz, " that there are some difficulties

in reconciling the name of Psammis with some
other monuments, and in particular with a most
important fragment of an enumeration of the
kings of Egypt, discovered by Mr. Bankes, at
Abydos. In this there are only two kings intervening between this Psammis and the Memnon
of the ancients: so that, if Pliny is right in his
account of this obelisc, the popular tradition
respecting the colossus, supposed to represent
Memnon, must be erroneous. This, indeed, it
would not be difficult to admit, as very likely to
have happened in the case of any popular tradition; but there is a still greater difficulty in the
inscription found by Mr. Bankes on the leg of
the colossus at Ebsambul, in which Psammetichus
is mentioned; and if this was the first Psammetichus, as appears in some respects to be the more
probable, it would follow that the king who
founded that temple was more ancient than
Psammetichus. But it is abundantly certain
that our Psammis was prior to the founder of
that temple: so that either that Psammetichus
must be of much later date, as the employment
of the Greek Ψ in the inscription would indeed
appear to indicate, or this catacomb was not constructed in honour of the son of Pharaoh Necho.
It has also been observed by an accomplished
scholar, who is much attached to the pursuit of
Egyptian antiquities, that, according to the testimony of Herodotus, all the kings of this dynasty

were buried at Saïs, and that we must either reject this evidence, or admit that neither Psammis nor Necho can be the personage here represented. We may, however, hope, that future researches will furnish us with materials, that may enable us to remove this and many other difficulties, which at present envelope the chronology of the kings of Egypt."

CHAPTER IV

ALTHOUGH the discovery of the general import of the hieroglyphics has by no means excited any great sensation in this country, yet the activity of the various collectors resident in Egypt seems to have been in some measure stimulated by it. Important additions have been made, or are about to be made, to the Egyptian department of the British Museum; and in France, the magnificent liberality of the Government, together with the insatiable curiosity of some affluent individuals, has held out ample encouragement to the commercial antiquarian.

I thought myself extremely fortunate, in my return from the short excursion to Rome and Naples, that I made in the autumn of 1821, to have discovered at Leghorn, among a multitude of Egyptian antiquities, belonging to Mr. Drovetti, the French consul at Alexandria, which had

long lain warehoused there, a stone containing
an enchorial and a Greek inscription, which was
known to have existed formerly at Menouf, but
which had been lost and almost forgotten by
European travellers in Egypt, and I believe by
Mr. Drovetti himself; for I am informed that it
is not mentioned in the catalogue of his Museum,
which has been sent to Paris and elsewhere.
Although both the inscriptions appeared to be almost illegible, yet I did not despair of being able,
in a proper light, and with sufficient patience,
to decipher the greater part; and I should have
been tempted to remain a few days at Leghorn,
in order to make the experiment, if I could have
obtained permission from the merchants, to whose
care the collection was entrusted. The more,
however, that I considered the importance of the
only supplement to the pillar of Rosetta, that
then appeared to be in existence, the more
anxiety I felt to make some effort, to secure it
from oblivion or destruction; and with more sim-
plicity, perhaps, than good policy, when I returned
to Pisa in the evening, I wrote a letter to MM.
Mompurgo, of which I shall here insert a translation.

" *Gentlemen,*

"Having fully reflected on the singular importance of the Greek inscription, which I mentioned
to you this morning, and the irreparable misfor-

tune that would be incurred, in case that the pillar containing it should ever be lost by shipwreck, I have determined to make you a proposal, which I hope you will not find any impropriety in accepting.

" I am very desirous of sending an experienced artist from Florence, in order to make two impressions in plaster, and two tracings on paper, of this stone; upon condition, that they be considered as the property of Mr. Drovetti, and remain in your possession, until you have received his answer to the inquiry, whether he will permit them to be sent to London, either for myself or for the British Museum, and what price he would expect to receive for them. And in case that he should not think proper to fix such a price on them, as we might agree to pay, I am willing to consent, that they should remain in his collection, upon condition, however, that if this collection should ever be reembarked, for conveyance by sea, they should be kept at Leghorn, until the original stone should have arrived safely at the place of its destination, in order to avoid the chance of wholly losing this literary treasure by shipwreck.

" Whatever may be Mr. Drovetti's decision, I trust that this application, from one who flatters himself that he is the only person living, that can fully appreciate the value of the object in question, will at least not be disagreeable to him. I

will beg of you to send me an early answer,
directed to Schneiderff's Hotel at Florence.

T. Y. Sec. R. S. Lond.

Pisa, 5th Sept. 1821."

MM. Mompurgo readily agreed to my proposal, and I engaged a distinguished artist of
Florence to undertake the performance of my
plan ; but I believe he was accidentally prevented
from fulfilling his engagement. It appears, however, that his labour, as far as I was concerned
would have been wholly lost; for Mr. Drovetti's
cupidity seems to have been roused by the discovery of an unknown treasure, and he has given
me to understand, that nothing should induce him
to separate it from the remainder of his extensive
and truly valuable collection, of which he thinks
it so well calculated to enhance the price; and
he refuses to allow any kind of copy of it to be
taken.

But, as it often happens to those who are too
eager to monopolize, he has now outstood his
market, and the pearl of great price, which six
months ago I would have purchased for much
more than its value, is now become scarcely
worth my acceptance. I was principally anxious
to obtain from it a collateral confirmation of my
interpretation of the enchorial inscription of Rosetta; but having fortunately acquired materials,
from other sources, which are amply sufficient

for this purpose, I can wait, with great patience, for any little extension, which my enchorial vocabulary might receive from this source. I had inferred from a note, that had been sent me several years before, respecting the stone of Menouf, by Mr. Jomard, that the first words of the Greek inscription must have been ΒΑΣΙΛΕΙ ΠΤΟΛΕΜΑΙΩΙ ΝΕΩΙ ΔΙΟΝΥΣΩΙ, but this was all that the gentleman, who described it, had even attempted to copy.

The first circumstance, that repressed my eagerness to obtain a copy of Drovetti's inscriptions, was the arrival of Mr. Casati at Paris, with a parcel of manuscripts, among which Mr. Champollion discovered one that considerably resembled, in its preamble, the enchorial text of the pillar of Rosetta: and the value of this discovery was afterwards almost miraculously multiplied, by the existence of a Greek translation of the same manuscript, which has been brought to London by Mr. Grey.

Having had occasion, in the month of September last, to accompany some friends in a short visit to Paris, I was very agreeably surprised with several literary and scientific novelties of uncommon interest, and all of them such as either had originated, or might have originated, from my own pursuits. I had first the pleasure of hearing, at a meeting of the Academy of Sciences, an optical paper read by Mr. Fresnel; who, though he appears to have rediscovered, by his own efforts,

the laws of the interference of light, and though he
has applied them, by some very refined calcula-
tions, to cases which I had almost despaired of
being able to explain by them, has, on all occasions, and particularly in a very luminous state-
ment of the theory, lately inserted in a translation
of Thomson's Chemistry, acknowledged, with the
most scrupulous justice, and the most liberal
candour, the indisputable priority of my investigations. In the course of the same week, I was
invited to sit next to Mr. Champollion junior,
while he was reading, to the Academy of Belles
Lettres, a Memoir on the Analysis of the Inscription of Rosetta: he, also, had been partly anticipated in his results by what had been done in this
country: though I could not help fancying, that
he had not so completely forgiven the injury, as
his countryman Mr. Fresnel appeared to have
done. But Mr. Fresnel is the friend of Arago,
and nothing more requires to be said of his character and sentiments.

I must, however, at once beg to be understood,
that I fully and sincerely acquit Mr. Champollion
of any intentions actually dishonourable: and if
I have hinted, that I have received an impression
of something like a want of liberality in his conduct, I have only thrown out this intimation, as
an apology for being obliged to plead my own
cause, and not as having any right to complain of
his silence, or as having any desire or occasion to

profit by his indulgence : at the same time I am
far from wishing to renounce his friendship, or to
forego the pleasure and advantage of his future
correspondence.

At the beginning of my Egyptian researches, I
had accidentally received a letter from Mr. Champollion, which accompanied a copy of his work
on the state of Egypt under the Pharaohs, sent as
a present to the Royal Society : and as he re-
quested some particular information respecting
several parts of the enchorial inscription of Rosetta, which were imperfectly represented in the
engraved copies, I readily answered his inquiries
from a reference to the original monument in the
British Museum : and a short time afterwards I
sent him a copy of my conjectural translation of
the inscriptions, as it was inserted in the Archaeologia.

Of Mr. Champollion's *Egypte sous les Pharaons*,
the two volumes, that have hitherto appeared,
relate only to the geography of ancient
Egypt, and especially to the determination of the
old Egyptian names of places, as compared with
the Greek and the Arabic, by the assistance of
Coptic manuscripts, and other intermediate documents.   The work exhibits considerable research,
and some ingenuity : the author had devoted his
life to one very extensive pursuit, and he proposed
to illustrate every part of his subject, by the most
minute investigation of every circumstance, that

could be brought to bear upon it. The undertaking, commenced on so large a scale, appears
to have proceeded but slowly ; nor is it probable
that the life of any man would be sufficient for its
complete execution. With regard to the enchorial Inscription, Mr.
Champollion appeared to me to have done at that
time but little. A few of the references, that he
made to it, seemed to depend entirely upon Mr.
Akerblad's investigations, although, as I have formerly had occasion to remark, it was *tacitly*
that he adopted Mr. Akerblad's conclusions. I
imagine, however, that he even now retains some
erroneous prepossessions, which he had imbibed
from Mr. Akerblad, although, very possibly, without recollecting their exact origin; in particular
respecting the adoption of some Greek epithets,
without translation, into the enchorial inscription :
this question, however, I trust is now set at rest,
by means of some later discoveries.

Mr. Champollion continued to reside at Grenoble, where he had some employment in the public
library, till the beginning of 1821. I had not a
convenient opportunity of sending him any of my
later papers ; and it was not till after he had left
Grenoble, that he read the Article EGYPT of the
Supplement of the Encyclopaedia, into which their
contents were condensed. He had been devoting
himself, in the mean time, to the uninterrupted
study of the enchorial inscription, and he ap-

pears to have discovered, before he came to Paris, the original identity of these characters with the imperfect imitations of the more distinct hierogly- phics. Whether he made this discovery before I had printed my letters in the Museum Criticum, I have no means of ascertaining: I have never asked him the question, nor is it of much conse- quence, either to the world at large or to our- selves. It may not be strictly just, to say, that a man has no right to claim any discovery as his own, till he has printed and published it : but the rule is at least a very useful one. It is always easy to publish such an account of a discovery, as to establish the right of originality, without affording much facility to the pursuits of a com- petitor : although it is generally true, that not only honesty, but even liberality, is the best policy.

Passing by, however, what I had already done, by far the most important to me was what I had not done, and there was enough of this to satisfy me, that Mr. Champollion was at least capable of doing many things, with respect to which his claim of actual priority might appear more than doubtful.

He had found, in the first place, among the multitude of Egyptian papyri, which he had taken the trouble to copy at length, with the permission of their various possessors, one in particular, of which a series of the chapters were pretty ob- viously numbered in the enchorial character, the

series extending, with a few interruptions, from
1 to 20. He had already applied this discovery
to the illustration. of some parts of the pillar of
Rosetta : and I have since derived at least equal
advantage from it, in the examination of the enchorial papyrus of Casati.

He had also discovered a fragment of a pillar
formerly in the possession of the Duc de Choiseul,
which exhibited the character for a month, followed
by several various groups, together with different
numbers, evidently indicative of days ; so that
to the names of the three months, which I had
discovered, he was enabled to add at least four
more, though without completely ascertaining to
which of the months these new symbols belonged.

Mr. Champollion had ascertained, in the third
place, the analogy of one of the manuscripts, purchased of Casati, to the enchorial inscription of
Rosetta, and he had obtained from it, without difficulty, the mode of writing the name Cleopatra in
that character. He did not, however, then mention to me the important consequences which he
had derived from this discovery; these, it seems,
were the subject of a short paper read to the Academy the succeeding Friday; and it will be proper to extract a more particular account of them,
from his Letter to Mr. Dacier, since printed ; in
which I did certainly expect to find the chronology of my own researches a little more distinctly
stated.

" The hieroglyphical text of the inscription of
Rosetta," he observes, (p. 6), " exhibited, on account of its fractures, *only the name of Ptolemy.*
The obelisc found in the Isle of Philae, and lately
removed to London, contains also the hieroglyphical name of *one of the Ptolemies,* expressed by
the same characters that occur in the inscription
of Rosetta, surrounded by a ring or border, and
it is followed by a second border, which must
necessarily contain the proper name of a woman,
and of a queen of the family of the Lagidae, since
this group is terminated by the hieroglyphics ex-
pressive of the *feminine* gender; characters which
are found at the end of the names of all the Egyptian goddesses without exception. The obelisc
was fixed, it is said, to a basis bearing a Greek
inscription, which is a petition of the priests of
Isis at Philae, addressed to King Ptolemy, to
Cleopatra his sister, and to Cleopatra his wife.
Now, if this obelisc, and the hieroglyphical inscription engraved on it, were the result of this
petition, which in fact adverts to the consecration
of a monument of the kind, the border, with the
feminine proper name, can only be that of one of
the Cleopatras. This name, and that of Ptolemy,
which in the Greek have several letters in common, were capable of being employed for a comparison of the hieroglyphical characters com-
posing them; and if the similar characters in
these names expressed in both the same sounds,

it followed that their nature must be entirely phonetic."

This course of investigation appears, indeed, to be so simple and so natural, that the reader must naturally be inclined to forget that any preliminary steps were required: and to take it for granted, either that it had long been known and admitted, that the rings on the pillar of Rosetta contained the name of Ptolemy, and that the semicircle and the oval constituted the female termination, or that Mr. Champollion himself had been the author of these discoveries.

It had, however, been one of the greatest difficulties attending the translation of the hieroglyphics of Rosetta, to explain how the groups within the rings, which varied considerably in different parts of the pillar, and which occurred in several places where there was no corresponding name in the Greek, while they were not to be found in others where they ought to have appeared, could possibly represent the name of Ptolemy; and it was not without considerable labour that I had been able to overcome this difficulty. The interpretation of the female termination had never, I believe, been suspected by any but myself: nor had the name of a single god or goddess, out of more than five hundred that I have collected, been clearly pointed out by any person.

But, however Mr. Champollion may have arrived at his conclusions, I admit them, ·with the
greatest pleasure and gratitude, not by any means
as superseding my system; but as fully confirming
and extending it. And here I am compelled to
advert to a note of Mr. Champollion's, which I fear
will be thought to go a little beyond a *tacit adoption* of my opinions, and to approach very near to
an unintentional misrepresentation. "It must,
without doubt, (p. 15,) have been by the form of
this symbol, which has some resemblance to the
figure of a basket, that Dr. Young was led to recognise the name of Berenice in the border that
actually contains it. But he was of opinion that
the hieroglyphics constituting proper names were
employed as expressing whole syllables, that they
were therefore a sort of *rebuses*, and that the first
character of the name of Berenice, for example,
represented the syllable BIR, which means a *basket*
in the Egyptian language. This mistaken supposition has vitiated, in great measure, the phonetic analysis which he has attempted of the names
of *Ptolemy* and *Berenice*, in which, notwithstanding, he has recognised the phonetic values of four
of the characters: these are the P, one of the
forms of the T, one of the forms of the M, and the
I; but the whole of his syllabic alphabet. established from these two names only, was completely
inapplicable to the great number of proper names

phonetically expressed on the various monuments
of Egypt...Encyclopaedia Britannica, Supplement,
IV. Pt. i. Edinb. Dec. 1819."

Now, if Mr. Champollion had attended to my
expressions, he must have perceived that it was
not by any *resemblance* of an imaginary nature that
I was " led to recognise the name of Berenice ; '
but by external evidence only. " The appellation
SOTERES," I have observed, Art. 57, " as a dual,
is well marked in the inscription of Rosetta, and
the character, thus determined, explains a long
name in the temple at Edfou..58. The wife of
Ptolemy Soter, and mother of Philadelphus, was
BERENICE, whose name is found on a ceiling at
KARNAK, in the phrase, " Ptolemy and .. Berenice, the *saviour gods*." In this name we appear
to have another specimen of syllabic *and alphabetical* writing combined, in a manner not extremely unlike the ludicrous mixtures of words
and things with which children are sometimes
amused; for however Warburton's indignation
might be excited by such a comparison, it is perfectly true that, occasionally, "the sublime differs
from the ridiculous by a single step only."..I
have then proceeded to state, as conjectural *inferences*, the syllabic analogies: but instead of
four letters which Mr. Champollion is pleased to
allow me, I have marked, in a subsequent chapter
of this Essay, *nine*, which I have actually specified
in different parts of my paper in the Supplement :

and to these he has certainly added *three* new ones; or *four*, if he chooses to reckon the E as a fourth. I allow that I suspected the B, the L, and the s, to be sometimes used syllabically : but the analogy of these characters, with the enchorial alphabet was so well marked, that my attempt to refine upon it could not easily have embarrassed any one in making the application. Mr. Champollion has never been led, in any one instance, from the Egyptian name of an object, to infer the phonetic interpretation, that is, the alphabetical power of its symbol: but the letters having once been ascertained, he has ransacked his memory or his dictionary for some name that he thought capable of being applied to the symbol: and not always, as it appears to me, in the most natural manner: I should prefer, for instance, the word HRERI, a flower, as making the R, to the name of pomegranate, which, it seems, was sometimes called ROMAN or ERMAN. I must also observe that my intention, in placing the Coptic names in my vocabulary of hieroglyphics, was to assist in tracing any such analogies that might suggest themselves: and in the instance of AM or EM, N.123, the reading approaches very near to one of the letters, added by Mr. Champollion to my alphabet.

With respect to the diversity of characters representing the same letter, it will be observed that I have marked *three* forms of the M, *three* of the N, with a fourth that was suggested to me by

Mr. Bankes, *two* of the P or PH, and *two* of the s. Of these last, I cannot omit to observe, that Mr. Champollion has devoted at least a page - of his letter (p. 13, 14) to the demonstration of the identity of *these same* forms : and that it would not have been unnatural to refer, in a single line of that page, to the assertion of the same identity, which I had made in the article EGYPT, No. 102. " The bent line is often exchanged in the manuscripts for the divided staff, and both are represented in the running hand by a figure like a 9 or a 4." The remainder of the forms, assigned to the letters, are all due to Mr. Champollion's ingenious and successful investigations.

It so happens, that in the lithographical sketch of the obelisc of Philae, which had been put into my hands by its adventurous and liberal possessor, the artist has expressed the first letter of the name of Cleopatra by a T instead of a K, and as I had not leisure at the time to enter into a very minute comparison of the name with other authorities, I suffered myself to be discouraged with respect to the application of my alphabet to its analysis, and contented myself with observing, that if the steps of the formation of an alphabet were not exactly such as I had pointed out, they must at least have been very nearly of the same nature. In return, I was complimented for my candour, while I ought, perhaps, to have been reproved for my timidity. If, however, I may judge from my

E

late correspondence with Mr Champollion, he
does not appear to be altogether so averse to the
admission of syllabic characters on some occasions, as his note upon my "false point of de-
parture" appears to imply: and I think he will
find, in the evidence now first made public, respecting the enchorial character, some additional
grounds for enforcing the opinion. I shall insert
a specimen of one variety of each of the names
which he has succeeded in deciphering: observing only, that his alphabet could scarcely have
agreed so well with the various combinations of
these names, as it appears to do, if it had not
been in great measure correct: and that I also
fully agree with Mr. Champollion in his interpretation of the phrase of the Pamfilian obelisc,
which he translates, WHO HAS RECEIVED THE
KINGDOM FROM VESPASIAN HIS FATHER: the same
phrase occurring on the pillar of Rosetta, as well
as on the obelisc of Philae, where it had served
to correct my later opinion respecting the symbol
for FATHER. It is here evident that the expression cannot relate, as Mr. St. Martin imagines it
must have done in the inscriptions of Rosetta, to
the immediate installation of a son by *the hands*
of his father; but that the right of inheritance only
was implied by it. I am not however convinced,
by the coherence of this passage, that the greater
part of the obelisc was ever intended by the
sculptor to convey a connected meaning; and at

any rate the explanation confirms the opinion, that
I had expressed, respecting the Roman origin of
the workmanship. There are a few of the busts,
now placed in the magical gallery of the Vatican,
which appeared to me, on the contrary, to have
been brought from Egypt with their genuine and
ancient inscriptions, and to have had their features newly formed, and more highly polished, by
Roman artists of the age of Adrian, in whose villa
at Tivoli they were principally found.

Mr. Champollion has lately had the goodness
to communicate to me, by letter, some suggestions,
which, I conclude, he is on the point of making
public, and I therefore take the liberty of men-
tioning them, as far as I think them at all admis-
sible, though, perhaps, a little prematurely. He
is disposed to refer the name, which I consider as
that of the father of Amasis, to SESOSTRIS, as
synonymous with RAMESSES, which he thinks the
characters are probably intended to express phonetically. Now I readily allow, that where this
name is written fully and accurately, as it is re-
peatedly found in Mr. Bankes's great catalogue of
Abydos, it may without much violence be read
nearly as Mr. Champollion proposes, " the ap-
proved by Phthah, Ramesses," or " the counter-
part of Phthah, Ramesses; " the first part of the
group undergoing several synonymous variations,
while the end remains unchanged ; although, if
this reading were established, I should refer the

first name to Amenophis or MEMNON, who was
the son of Ramesses, or of Armesses called
Miamun; and to whom the tomb of my Amasis
is said to be attributed in the Greek and Latin
inscriptions which are found in it; who is also
said to have built the palace of Abydos, on which
my Amasis evidently appears as the founder; who
is more easily understood than Amasis to be prior
to the Psammetichus mentioned at Ebsambul;
and, who is more likely than Amasis to have been
at Berytus, or Nahr el Kelb, where Mr. Wyse, as
I am informed by Sir William Gell, has distinctly
observed this name, accompanied by the nail-
headed characters. All these reasons are more
than sufficient to counterbalance the single assertion of Pliny; and we should be obliged to
change my Psammis, according to his place in
Mr. Bankes's table of kings, into the Armais of
Manetho; though the *vocal* Memnon of the numerous inscriptions would be converted by this
comparison into Queen Rathotis, or we should
be obliged to leave out three of Manetho's list, to
bring him up to the Amenophis who is called the
Trojan Memnon by that author. All this is, indeed, a little alluring, and several suppositions
might be int oduced to overcome the difficulties:
but unfortu ately the fundamental supposition
appears to be liable to an insurmountable objec-
tion; that the circle, which Mr. Champollion
considers as equivalent to the RE or RA of Rames-

ses, is also the first character of each of the seven-
teen names immediately preceding it, and indeed
of every other in the catalogue, that remains un-
mutilated at the beginning.

I am therefore sorry to say that I cannot hitherto
congratulate Mr. Champollion on the success of
his attempts to carry his system of phonetic characters into the very remotest antiquity of Egypt:
he appears, however, to have a better prospect
of elucidating some of the Persian names, having,
as he informs me, been able to identify that of
XERXES, both in the hieroglyphics, and in the nail-
headed characters, by means of a vase of alabaster,
on which both are found together. This is, indeed, a wonderful opening for literary enterprise;
and I am even inclined to hope, from Mr. Champollion's latest communications, that he will find
some means of overcoming the difficulties that I
have stated respecting the Pharaohs, for he as-
sures me, that he has identified the names of no
less than THIRTY of them, and that they accord
with the traditions of Manetho, and, as far as he
can judge, with the notes that I had sent him of
an attempt that I had formerly made to assign
temporary names to the kings enumerated at
Abydos, in which those of all the later ones
began with the syllable RE. He will easily believe that I wish for a satisfactory answer to my
own objections: and, in fact, the further that he
advances by the exertion of his own talents and

ingenuity, the more easily he will be able to admit, without any exorbitant sacrifice of his fame, the claim that I have advanced to a priority with respect to the first elements of all his researches; and I cannot help thinking that he will ultimately feel it most for his own substantial honour and reputation, to be more anxious to admit the just claims of others than they can be to advance them.

CHAPTER V.

ILLUSTRATIONS OF THE MANUSCRIPTS BROUGHT
FROM EGYPT BY MR. GREY.

I AM impatient to turn, from every thing of a polemical or personal nature, to a field that has hitherto been exclusively in my own possession, in consequence of an event, which is the most important, considered as a single occurrence, that has taken place since the commencement of my Egyptian researches. It was very soon after my return from France, that George Francis Grey, Esq. of University College, Oxford, having been at Naples upon his return from Egypt, was so good as to bring me a few lines from my old friend Sir William Gell, himself a very successful traveller, and who has always pursued with ardour the last vestiges of the interesting remains of antiquity, both by his personal exertions, and by assisting and directing the enterprises of others.

Mr. Grey had the kindness, on the 22d of November last, to leave with me a box, containing several fine specimens of writing and drawing on papyrus; they were chiefly in hieroglyphics, and of a mythological nature: but the two which he had before described to me, as particularly deserving attention, and which were brought, through his judicious precautions, in excellent preservation, both contained some Greek characters, written apparently in a pretty legible hand. He had purchased them of an Arab at Thebes, in January 1820; and that which was most intelligible had appeared, at first sight, to contain some words relating to the service of the Christian church. Mr. Grey was so good as to give me leave to make any use of these manuscripts that I pleased ; and he readily consented to their insertion among the lithographic copies of the " Hieroglyphics, collected by the Egyptian Society," which I had undertaken to superintend from time to time, in great measure for the private use of an association of my own friends, not sufficiently numerous to insure any permanent stability to its continuance.

Mr. Champollion had done me the favour, while I was at Paris, to copy for me some parts of the very important papyrus, which I have before mentioned as having given him the name of Cleopatra; and of which the discovery was certainly a great event in Egyptian literature, since it was the first time that any intelligible characters, of the enchorial form, had been discovered among the many manuscripts and inscriptions that had been examined, and since it furnished Mr. Champollion at the same time with a name, which materially advanced,

if I understood him rightly, the steps that have led
him to his very important extension of the hieroglyphical alphabet. He had mentioned to me, in con-
versation, the names of Apollonius, " Antiochus,"
and Antigonus, as occurring among the witnesses ;
and I easily recognised the groups which he had
deciphered : although, instead of *Antiochus,* I read
Antimachus ; and I did not recollect at the time
that he had omitted the M.

In the evening of the day that Mr. Grey had
brought me his manuscripts, I proceeded impa-
tiently to examine that which was in Greek only :
and I could scarcely believe that I was awake,
and in my sober senses, when I observed, among
the names of the witnesses, ANTIMACHUS ANTIGE-
NIS : and, a few lines further back, PORTIS APOL-
LONII ; although the last word could not have
been very easily deciphered, without the assistance of the conjecture, which immediately occurred to me, that this manuscript might perhaps be
a translation of the enchorial manuscript of Casati :
I found that its beginning was, " A copy of an
Egyptian writing...; " and I proceeded to ascertain, that there were the same number of names,
intervening between the Greek, and the Egyptian
signatures, that I had identified, and that the same
number followed the last of them ; and the whole
number of witnesses appeared to be sixteen in
each. The last paragraph in the Greek began
with the words, " Copy of the Registry ; " for such

must be the signification of the word ΠΤΩΜΑΤΟΣ,
employed in this papyrus, though it does not appear to occur any where else in a similar signification. I could not, therefore, but conclude, that
a most extraordinary chance had brought into my
possession a document which was not very likely,
in the first place, ever to have existed, still less to
have been preserved uninjured, for my information, through a period of near two thousand years:
but that this very extraordinary translation should
have been brought safely to Europe, to England,
and to me, at the very moment when it was most
of all desirable to me to possess it, as the illustration of an original which I was then studying,
but without any other reasonable hope of being
able fully to comprehend it; this combination
would, in other times, have been considered as
affording ample evidence of my having become an
Egyptian sorcerer.

Mr. Champollion had not thought it worth while
to give me a transcript of the original Greek en-
dorsement: he seemed to consider it as not fully
agreeing with the Egyptian text, or, at any rate,
as not materially assisting in its interpretation:
perhaps, also, he thought it best for me to try my
strength upon the original, without any little assistance that might have been derived from it
with respect to two or three of the names: or, as
I am more disposed to believe, he was fearful of
offending some of his countrymen, by making too

public what he had no right to communicate without their leave: for after an accidental delay of a month, the answer that I received from Paris was only such as to enable me to state, that my opinion of the identity of the two endorsements is fully confirmed. I have lost, however, no time in sending to the Conservators of the King's cabinet a copy of my registry; with a request to be favoured with theirs in return, in order that I might have the same advantage from the comparison, which I voluntarily afforded the Parisian critics, without any reserve or delay ; and in order that the duplicates may stand side by side in the lithographical copy, which has only waited for their answer, to have a vacant space filled up, and to be sent to them entire. In the mean time, I have only to wish, that the philologists of Paris may do as ample justice to these papyri, as one of the most distinguished of their number, Mr. Letronne, has lately done to the inscriptions of the Oasis, of which I had made a very hasty translation from a single copy only, not having had the means of comparing it properly with the second.

My application for the copy of the Registry has been received with the liberality which was to be expected from the directors of a great institution, and I have to return my best thanks to Mr. Raoul Rochette, for a correct copy of the whole of this highly important manuscript, which I am happy to find that it is his intention to publish in a short time.

I am most anxious to avoid anticipating him, in the gratification of the public curiosity, with regard to this interesting relic: but as I find that some account of the Registry has already been made public by Mr. St. Martin, I conceive myself at liberty to make use, at least, of this part of the manuscript: and I do not imagine that Mr. Raoul Rochette means to employ himself on the enchorial conveyance.

The contents of Mr. Grey's Greek manuscript are of a nature scarcely less remarkable than its preservation and discovery: it relates to the sale, not of a house or a field, but of a portion of the Collections and Offerings made from time to time on account, or for the benefit, of a certain number of MUMMIES, of persons described at length, in very bad Greek, with their children and all their households. The price is not very clearly expressed; but as the portion sold is only a moiety of a third part of the whole, and as the testimony of sixteen witnesses was thought necessary on the occasion, it is probable that the revenue, thus obtained by the priests, was by no means inconsiderable.

The result, derived at once from this comparison, is the identification of more than thirty proper names as they were written in the running hand of the country. It might appear, upon a superficial consideration, that a mere catalogue of proper names would be of little comparative value in assisting us to recover the lost elements of a language. But, in fact, they possess a considerable advantage, in the early stages of such an investigation, from the greater facility and certainty with which they are identified, and from their independence of any grammatical inflexions, at least in the present case; by means of which they lead us immediately to a full understanding of the orthographical system of the language, where any such system can be traced.

The general inference, to be derived from an examination of the names now discovered, is somewhat more in favour of an extensive employment of an alphabetical mode of writing, than any that could have been deduced from the pillar of Rosetta, which exhibits, indeed, only foreign names, and affords us therefore little or no information respecting the mode of writing the original Egyptian names of the inhabitants. Several of the words, which occur in these documents, and more especially in those which are hereafter to be mentioned, might be read pretty correctly, by means of the alphabet originally made out by Mr. Akerblad from the foreign names of the enchorial inscription; but there are many more which appear to be rather syllabically than alphabetically constituted: and the names of the different deities seem to be very commonly employed in writing them; for instance, those of Horus, Ammon, and Isis; and perhaps in the same way that they are often composed, in the mythological manuscripts, found with the mummies: in which, for want of the occurrence of a ring or border, or of the corresponding enchorial marks, I had concluded that the groups could not be intended to represent the ordinary names of the individuals. But these marks are, in fact, by no means constantly employed in the enchorial papyri; and they seem only to have been inserted when either great precision, or some distinguished mark of respect was required.

Important, however, as are the additions that are likely to be made to our knowledge by means of this "Antigraph", it is by no means the only valuable acquisition for which we are indebted to the enterprise and the diligence of Mr. Grey: a second papyrus, of considerably greater magnitude, contains three Egyptian conveyances in the enchorial character, with separate registries on the margin, in very legible Greek. These are not only of use for the illustration of other similar documents, but they afford us also many additional examples of enchorial proper names, besides a general idea of the subjects of the respective manuscripts, all of which relate to the sale of lands in the neighbourhood of Thebes. It will be most convenient to consider them as parts of a series, of which those are the first to be examined, that are the most capable of affording an independent testimony; beginning with the Greek papyrus in

the possession of Mr. Anastasy, the Swedish consul at Alexandria, and proceeding to the Antigraph
and its original, and thence to the three enchorial
manuscripts, which are also the property of Mr.
Grey. It is scarcely conceivable, by a person
who has not made the experiment; how much
the difficulty of reading a depraved character is
almost universally diminished by the comparison
of two or three copies of the same or of similar
passages; the words, which would be wholly un-
intelligible in either taken singly, being often very
easily legible when both are at once under the eye;
and, still more commonly, a word which is confused
or contracted in one, being written clearly or at
length in another.

It is in this manner, that several of the defi-
ciencies of the manuscript of Anastasy, as edited
by the learned and ingenious Professor Bockh of
Berlin, have been in some measure supplied, in
the late republication at Paris, by the care of Mr.
Jomard, from a comparison with the Greek manuscripts purchased of Mr. Casati, in order to be
added to the unrivalled treasures of literature
contained in the King's library and cabinet. Several more of the obscurities of this manuscript,
if not the whole, I flatter myself are now removed,
by the further comparison, which I have attempted
to make, by means of Mr. Grey's indulgence in
allowing me the use of his manuscripts; and
by means of the duplicate which I have received

from Paris in exchange for the registry of his
Antigraph.

The manuscript of Anastasy, besides its curiosity as a subject of antiquarian and historical
research, becomes of great importance, in this
inquiry, as affording a more complete specimen,
than the Antigraph, of the usual form of a contract
in Egypt under the Ptolemies; and as assisting
in the investigation of the sense of the preamble
of the enchorial manuscript, which is omitted in
the Antigraph. I shall therefore insert here a
translation of this document, and shall reprint the
original in an appendix, with such corrections as
I have thought it appeared to require; in order
to restore it to the form intended by the writer.
The registries, in their original language, I shall
print side by side, and in the order of time which
I attribute to them.

TRANSLATION OF THE GREEK PAPYRUS OF
ANASTASY.

See Appendix I.

(1) In the reign of Cleopatra and Ptolemy her
son surnamed Alexander, the Gods Philometores
Soteres, in the year XII, otherwise IX; in the
priesthood of the existing priests (2) in Alexandria, [the priest] of Alexander and of the Gods
Soteres, and of the Gods Adelphi, and of the Gods
Evergetae, and of the Gods Philopatores, and of
the Gods Epiphanes, and of the God (3) Philometor, and of the God Eupator, and of the Gods
Evergetae: the Prize bearer of Berenice Evergetis, the Basket bearer of Arsinoe Philadelphus
and the priestess of Arsinoe (4) Eupator at present in Alexandria: and, in the Thebaic Ptolemais,
in the priesthood of the existing priests and
priestesses of Ptolemy Soter, [and of ...] (5) in
Ptolemais; on the 29th of the month Tybi [v;
February]: Apollonius being President of the
Exchange of the Memnonians, and of the lower
government of the Pathyritic nome.

(6) There was sold by Pamonthes, aged about
45, of middle size, dark complexion, and hand-
some figure, bald, round faced, and straight nosed;
and by Snachomneus, aged about 20, of middle
size, sallow complexion, (7) likewise round faced

F

and straight nosed; and by Semmuthis Persineï, aged about 22, of middle size, sallow complexion, round faced, flat nosed, and of quiet demeanour; and by Tathlyt (8) Persinei, aged about 30, of middle size, sallow complexion, round face, and straight nose, with their principal Pamonthes, a party in the sale; the four (9) being of the children of Petepsais of the leather cutters of the Memnonia; out of the piece of level ground which belongs to them in the southern part of the Memnonia, (10) eight thousand cubits of open field, one fourth [of the whole?] bounded on the south by the Royal Street; on the north and east by the land of Pamonthes and Boconsiemis, who is his brother, (11) and the common land [or wall] of the city; on the west by the house of Tages the son of Chalome: a canal running through the middle, leading from the river: these are the neighbours on all sides. It was bought by Nechutes the less, (12) the son of Asos, aged about 40, of middle size, sallow complexion, cheerful countenance, long face, and straight nose, with a scar upon the middle of his forehead; for 601 pieces of brass: the sellers standing as (13) brokers, and as securities for the validity of the sale. It was accepted by Nechutes the purchaser.

APOLLONIUS Pr. Exch?

[REGISTRY.]

In the year XII, otherwise IX ; the 20th of
Pharmuthi [VIII ; May], [transacted] at the table
in Hermopolis, at which Dionysius presides, over
the 20th department; in the account of the partners receiving the duties on sales, of which He-
raclides is the subscribing clerk, the acceptor in
in the sale is Nechutes the less, the son of Asos ;
an open field of eight thousand cubits, one fourth
portion; in the southern part of the Memnonia :
which he bought of Pamonthes and Snachomneus,
the sons of Petepsais, with their sisters : 601 pieces ?
The end ...

Dionysius subscribes.

The beginning of this preamble may be illustrated by that of the inscription of ROSETTA,
which runs nearly thus :

In the reign of the young king.. Ptolemy Epiphanes the munificent.. the son of Ptolemy and
Arsinoe, the gods Philopatores.. in the year IX ;
the priest of Alexander and of the gods Soteres, and
of the gods Adelphi, and of the gods Evergetae, and
of the gods Philopatores, and of the god Epiphanes
the munificent being Aetus, the son of Aetus : the
prize bearer of Berenice Evergetis being Pyrrha
the daughter of Philinus : the basket bearer of
Arsinoe Philadelphus being Areia daughter of
Diogenes ; and the priestess of Arsinoe Philo-

pator, Irene the daughter of Ptolemy : on the
4th day of Xanthicus, or the 18th of Mechir : it
was decreed...

In comparing the preamble of the deed of sale
with this monument, we have first to observe the
successive addition of the names of Philometor,
Eupator, and the Evergetae, to the titles of the
priests of Alexander and his successors. Eupator,
it seems, according to other authorities, cited by
Bockh, was Ptolemy Evergetes II, the successor
of Philometor, called also Cacergetes and Physcon; and the Evergetae, named after him, can
only have been the reigning sovereigns, before
called Philometores Soteres: and Cleopatra, at
least, had some right to the name Evergetis, as having derived it from her husband, so that she may
easily be supposed to have shared it occasionally
with her son. The remaining part of the preamble varies but little, except that Arsinoe, instead
of Philopator, is called Eupator : but this diversity is not more material than the substitution of
Adelphi for Philadelphi, which frequently occurs.
The double date is well known to have been
adopted by Cleopatra and Alexander, and its origin is sufficiently explained by Eusebius and
Porphyry. Professor Böckh makes the year, 104
B. C. ; but from a comparison of different authorities it seems rather more probable that it was 106
B. C., at least so I have been obliged to arrange
it in a table, formed from a comparison of the chro-

nologies of Porphyry, Champollion Figeac, and St. Martin, which I have inserted in an Appendix.

TRANSLATION OF MR. GREY'S GREEK ANTIGRAPH.

(1) *Copy of an Egyptian Writing respecting the Dead Bodies in Thyn. having been* (2) *ratif* . . .

(3) In the XXXVIth year; Athyr [III] 20, after the usual preamble, this writing witnesses: that the ¿ Dresser? (4) among the servants of the great goddess [Isis?] Onnophris the son of Horus and of Senpoeris ,[aged about] forty, lively, tall, of a sallow complexion, hollow eyed, (5) and bald, has ceded voluntarily for the price of .. to Horus the son of Horus and of Senpoeris, (6) one moiety of the third part of the Collection for the dead (7) lying in Thynabunun, on the Libyan side of the Theban suburb, (8) in the Memnonia: likewise one moiety of the third part of the Services or Liturgies (9) and so forth: their names being | Muthes the son of Spotus, with (10) his children (10) and all his household; Chapocrates the son of Nechthmonthes, with his children and all; Arsiesis the son of Nechthmonthes; likewise Petemestus the son of (11) Nechthmonthes; likewise Arsiesis the son of Zminis; likewise (12) Osoroeris the son of [Horus]; likewise Spotus the

son of Chapochonsis ; likewise (13) Zoglyphus :
from which there belongs to Asos the son of Horus
and of Senpoeris (14) " thy" younger brother, one
of [or, the younger brother of] the same ¿ Dressers ?
a moiety of the (15) aforesaid third part of the
services and fruits and (16) so forth. He has sold it
to him in the year XXXVI ; 20 Athyr,in the reign of
the everlasting (17) king, for the completion of the
third part.   Also a moiety of the fruits (18)¿ and
so forth ? of the ¿ other ? dead bodies in Thy. that is
to say, Pateutemis with his children and (19) all ;
and a moiety of the fruits belonging to me from the
property of (20) Petechonsis the milk bearer, and
from a place on the Asiatic side, called (21) Phrecages, with the dead bodies in it ; of which a
moiety belongs to the (22) same Asos : all these
things I have sold to him.   They are thine, (23)
and I have received their price from thee, and I
make no demand upon thee (24) for them from
this day : and if any person disturb thee (25) in
the possession of them, I will withstand the attempt, and if I do not [otherwise] repel it (26) I
will use compulsory means.   Written by Horus
the son of Phabis, the writer of the (27) [priests]
of Amonrasonther, and the other gods of the temple. (28) Witnesses : Erieus the son of Phanres.
Peteartres the son of Pateutemis. (29)   Petearpocrates the son of [Horus]. Snachomneus the son
of Peteuris. Snachomes (30) the son of Psenchonsis.
Totoes the son of Phibis.   Portis the son of

APOLLONIUS. Zminis (31) the son of Petemestus. Peteutemis the son of Arsiesis. Amonorytius (32) the son of Pacemis. Horus the son of Chimnaraus. Armenis the son of Zthenaetis (33). Maesis the son of Mirsis. ANTIMACHUS the son of ANTIGENES. Petophois the son of Phibis. (34) Panas the son of Petosiris. Witnesses 16.

Copy of the Registry. In the year XXXVI; the ninth of Choeak [IV]. Transacted at the table in Diospolis, at which Lysimachus is the President of the 20th department; in the account of Asclepiades and Zminis, farmers of the tax, in which the subscribing clerk is Ptolemaeus : the purchaser Horus the son of Horus the ¿ Dresser ? a part of the sum, collected by them, on account of the dead bodies lying in Thynabunun, in the Memnonian tombs of the Libyan suburb of Thebes, for the services which are performed. Bought of Onnophris the son of Horus, Pieces of brass 400 . Z . . The end.

Lysimach. subscribes.

TRANSLATION OF THE ENCHORIAL PAPYRUS OF
PARIS, CONTAINING THE ORIGINAL DEED RE-
LATING TO THE MUMMIES.

(1) This writing, dated in the year XXXVI;
Athyr 20, in the reign of our Sovereigns Ptolemy
and Cleopatra his sister, the children of Ptolemy
and Cleopatra, the divine, (2) the Gods Illustrious: and the Priest of Alexander, and of the
Saviour Gods, of the Brother Gods, of the [Bene-
ficent Gods], of the Father loving Gods, of the
Illustrious Gods, of the Paternal God, and (3) of
the Mother loving Gods being [as by law ap-
pointed]: and the Prize bearer of Berenice the
Beneficent, and the Basket bearer of Arsinoe the
Brother loving, and the Priestess of (4) Arsinoe
the Father loving, being as appointed in the metropolis [of Alexandria]; and in [Ptolemaïs] the
Royal City ¿ of the Thebaid? the Guardian
Priest ¿ for the year? of Ptolemy Soter, and
the Priest of King Ptolemy the Father loving,
(5) and the Priest of Ptolemy the Brother
loving, and the Priest of Ptolemy the Beneficent, and the Priest of Ptolemy the Mother
loving; and the Priestess of Queen Cleopatra,
and the Priestess (6) of the Princess Cleopatra, and the Priestess of Cleopatra the [Queen]
Mother, deceased, the Illustrious; and the Basket
bearer of Arsinoe the Brother loving, [being as

appointed]: declares: The ¿Dresser? in the temple
(7) of the Goddess, Onnophris the son of Horus,
and of Senpoeris ¿ daughter of Spotus? [" aged
about forty, lively"], tall, [" of a sallow complexion, hollow eyed, and bald"]: in the temple
of the goddess (8) to [Horus] ¿ his brother? the
son of Horus and of Senpoeris, has sold, for a price
in money, half of one third of the Collections for
the dead, " Priests of Osiris ?" lying (9) in Thynabunun . . . in the Libyan suburb of Thebes, in
the Memnonia . . . likewise half of one third of
the Liturgies: their names being, Muthes the son
of Spotus, with his children and his household;
Chapocrates (10) the son of Nechthmonthes, with
his children and his household; Arsiesis the son
of Nechthmonthes, with his children and his
household; Petemestus the son of Nechthmonthes,
Arsiesis the son of Zminis, with his children and
his household; Osoroeris (11) the son of Horus,
with his children and his household; Spotus the
son of Chapochonsis ¿ surnamed? Zoglyphus [the
Sculptor,] with his children and his household :
while there belonged also to Asos the son of Horus and of Senpoeris ¿ daughter of Spotus? (12)
in the same manner one half of a third of the collections for the dead, and of the fruits and so
forth . . : he sold it on the 20th of Athyr, in the
reign of the king everliving, to [complete] the third
part : likewise the half ¿ of one third? of the collections relating to (13) Peteutemis, with his

household and . . : likewise the half ¿ of one
third? of the collections and fruits for Petechonsis the bearer of milk, and of the . . place
on the Asian side called Phrecages (14), and . .
and the dead bodies in it: there having belonged
to Asos the son of Horus one half of the same :
he has sold to him in the month of . . the half of
one third of the collections (15) for the Priests ¿
of Osiris? lying in Thynabunun, with their children and their households: likewise the half of
one third of the collections for Peteutemis, and
also for (16) Petechonsis the bearer of milk,
in the place Phrecages on the Asian side: I have
received for them their price in silver : . . and
gold : . . and I make no further demand on thee
for them from the present day, . . (17) . . before the authorities . . [and if any one shall disturb thee in the possession of them, I will resist
him, and if I do not succeed, I will indemnify
thee?] . . (18) Executed and confirmed : Written
by Horus the son of Phabis, clerk to the chief
priests of Amonrasonther and of the ¿ contemplar?
Gods, of the Beneficent Gods, of the Father
loving Gods, of the Paternal God, and of the (19)
Mother loving Gods. Amen. (20) Names of
the witnesses present. . .

[*Column at the edge of the paper.*] (1) Names
of the authorities. (2) Erieus the son of Phanres
¿ Erieus? (3) Peteartres the son of Peteutemis. (4)
Petearpocrates the son of Horus. (5) Snachomneus

the son of Peteuris. (6) Snachomes the son of
Psenchonsis. (7) Totoes the son of Phibis. (8)
Portis the son of APOLLONIUS. (9) Zminis the
son of Petemestus. (10) Peteutemis the son of
Arsiesis. (11) Amonorytius the son of Pacemis.
(12) Horus the son of Chimnaraus. (13) Armenis
[rather Arbais,]the son of Zthenaetis. (14) Maesis
the son of Mirsis. (15) ANTIMACHUS the son of
ANTIGENES. (16) Petophois the son of Phibis. (17)
Panas the son of Petosiris. (18) Were present
[as witnesses.]

The additions to the Sovereigns, named in the
preamble of the stone of Rosetta, are here the Paternal God and the Mother loving Gods, or Eupator and the Philometores, and we want only the
Evergetae of the papyrus of Anastasy. We can,
therefore, only refer the date to one of the two
preceding reigns, of Philometor or Evergetes Eupator, which it is very difficult to distinguish
from each other with precision. We have, however, no evidence that Philometor's dates extended beyond 35, and we must naturally consider this 36 as belonging to Eupator, corresponding to 135 B. C. which was 11 years after
the death of Philometor. If we judged from this
manuscript alone, we should infer that Eupator
was canonized, by some accident, during his temporary reign, before his brother, and that the order of the names remained undisturbed through
the different changes of their governments. The

epithet " Illustrious" in this preamble is not
easily recognised ; but it is distinguished by the
termination from " Beneficent," for which I
had in the first instance mistaken it: an epithet
so placed is almost always referred to the person
last mentioned. The enchorial name of the divinity here called Amonrasonther considerably resembles that of the " Cerexochus" of the Article
Egypt. The epithet, which I have conjecturally
translated " Dresser", was at first supposed to
mean Brazier, and was read Chalchytes: but the
Parisian Registry has distinctly Cholchytes:
which may possibly be a derivative of DCHOLH
or JOLH, to dress, to put on, and may have been
applied to some of the Hierostolists, or Tire
men, of the temple.

TRANSLATION OF MR. GREY'S ENCHORIAL PAPYRUS.

REGISTRY IN GREEK (A).

In the year XXVIII; the 28 Mesore [XII].
Transacted at the table in Hermopolis, at
which Dio.[nysius] is President of the 20th
department, in the Account of Asclepiades
[contractor for the tax] on sales; of which
Ptolemaeus is the subscribing clerk : the purchaser being Teephbis the son of Amenothes ¿
for 300 pieces of brass? ¿ of 7000? cubits, at the
southern end of the whole open field, which is at
the south of Diospolis the Great; of which the

boundaries are given in the annexed agreement :
which he bought of Alecis and Lubais and Tbaeais
the sons of Erieus, and of Senerieus the daughter
of Petenephotes, and Erieus the son of Amenothes,
and Senosorphibis the daughter of Amenothes,
and of Spois also ¿ the son? of Erieus the son of
Amenothes.   In the XXVIIIth year, Pachon [ix]
20. ¿ Pieces?.. End of the record.

Dionysius has subscribed.

ENCHORIAL AGREEMENT (A).

Year XXVIII; Month . . . In the reign of
Ptolemy and Cleopatra his sister, the children of
Ptolemy and Cleopatra, the Illustrious Gods:
and the Priest of Alexander, of the Saviour Gods,
of the ¿ Maternal? [Brother] Gods, of the Beneficent Gods, of the Father loving Gods, of the Il·
lustrious Gods, of the Mother loving Gods: and
the Prize bearer of Berenice the Beneficent, and
the Basket bearer of Arsinoe the Brother loving,
and the Priest of Arsinoe the Father loving, being
as appointed in the metropolis [of Alexandria; and
in Ptolemais], the Royal City ¿ of the Thebaid?
the Guardian Priest ¿ for the year? of Ptolemy
Soter, and the Priest of Ptolemy the Mother loving, and the Priest of Ptolemy the Brother loving,
and the Priest of Ptolemy the Beneficent, and the
Priest of Ptolemy the Father loving, and the Priest
of Ptolemy the Illustrious and Munificent, and the

Priest of Queen Cleopatra, and the Priest of Cleopatra the Mother, the late Goddess Illustrious; and the Basket bearer of Arsinoe the Brother loving, being [all as by law appointed]: The brothers, Alecis the son of Erieus, Lubais the son of Erieus, and Tbaeais the son of Erieus, their mother being Senerieus the daughter of Petenephotes son of Lubais; Erieus the son of Amenothes, and Senosorphibis daughter of Amenothes, whose mother was Senamunis, and Spois the son of Erieus, the son of Amenothes, his mother being ¿ Senchonsis? coming into the temple of ¿ Thebes? agreed with Teephbis son of Amenothes, to sell for a sum of money . . *α* . . *α* . . *α* . . *α* . . of the city . . in the year and month and day [above mentioned] of the King everliving . . *α* . . ¿ Alecis Phaïne? . *α* . . (16) *α* . . Asos the son of Horus and of Senpoeris . . the Royal Street (HIR = *ῥύμη*) . . ¿ vineyard? . . *α* . . *α* . . (19) . . (20) . . place . . (21) given up . . month . . time . . (22) . . (23) . . (24) . . Executed and confirmed. Written by Erieus the son of Phanres, clerk to the chief Priests of Amonrasonther and the contemplar Gods . . Amen.

It is sufficiently obvious that this deed must belong to the same period as the sale of the collections for the mummies, and that it must consequently have been at least eight years earlier. The " God Eupator" is here omitted, perhaps accidentally, or perhaps because he had not been canonized at the time. The date 28 is equally applicable to the reigns of Philometor and of Eupator : and several names occur in this deed which are also found in the preceding : for example, Erieus the son of Phanres, who is the first witness in that deed, is the clerk that drew up the present. Asos the son of Horus and Senpoeris, who is one of the "Dressers" of the temple, appears here as the possessor, probably of a neighbouring piece of land, and in the next deed as a purchaser. The question remains whether we should assign to this deed a date 19 years earlier than the former, or only 8, that is, whether 154 B. C. or 143; and there appears to be no evidence at present existing that is sufficient to decide it : except that the omission of the name of Eupator was less likely to happen in his own reign than in his predecessor's. The priesthoods of Ptolemais are somewhat negligently arranged at the end of this preamble, but they present no essential discordances. The Registry affords us a remarkable instance of a double contraction for the word ΠΟΛΙΣ or city, it is first represented by a semicircle with a central point, ⊙, and then by a figure of 2, in the names of Hermopolis, and Diospolis, or Thebes. The contraction for Hermopolis, in the papyrus of Anastasy, would not easily have been explained without the aid of these manuscripts. The Dionysius of the reign of Ptolemy Alexander, being near fifty years

later, may perhaps have been a son of this Dionysius, and may have succeeded him in his office.

TRANSLATION OF THE SECOND DEED (B).

REGISTRY, IN GREEK.

In the year **XXIX**; Phamenoth [vii] 9. Transacted at the table in Hermopolis, at which Dionysius is president of the 20th department; in the
account of Asclepiades and Crates [contractors for
the duties] on sales, of which Ptolemaeus is the
subscribing clerk : Asus, the son of Horus, purchaser of an open field of ¿ 2000 ? [square cubits],
lying in the southern part of Diospolis the Great;
of which the boundaries are given in the present
agreement: which he bought of Alecis the son of
Erieus, and Lubais and Tbaeais the sons of Erieus,
and Senerieus the daughter of Petenephotes, and
Erieus the son of Amenothes, and Senosorphibis
the daughter of Amenothes, and Spois [or Spoetus]
also the son of Erieus the son of Amenothes . .
¿ Pieces . . 1004 ? The end . . .

  Diony[sius] has subscribed.

ENCHORIAL AGREEMENT (B).

Year **XXIX**. In the reign of Ptolemy and Cleopatra, the children of Ptolemy and Cleopatra the
Gods Illustrious and Munificent: living for ever.

The brothers, Alecis the son of Erieus, Lubais the son of Erieus, and Tbaeais the son of Erieus, their mother being Senerieus the daughter of Petenephotes, son of Lubais; Erieus the son of Amenothes, and Senosorphibis daughter of Amenothes, her mother being Senamunis, and ¿ Spois? the son of Erieus, the son of Amenothes, his mother being ¿ Senchonsis? coming into the temple of ¿ Thebes? agreed with Asus the son of Horus to sell for a sum of money .. *α* .. *κ* .. *κ* .. *α* .. of the city .. in the year and month and day [above mentioned] of the king everliving .. *α*   .. ¿ Phaine? .. *α* .. the Royal Street; ¿ the sister of Alecis, Phaine? .. *α* .. *α* .. place .. has released .. months .. time .. Executed and confirmed. Written by Erieus the son of Phanres, clerk to the chief priests of Amonrasonther and the contemplar Gods ... Amen.

The preamble is here abridged, which was perhaps the safer, as the deed stands by the side of the preceding on the same papyrus. The phrase "*α*" is the same in both deeds, and probably means " a piece of open field bounded by," or something of a similar nature: for forms of this kind appear to be repeated without limit in the old Egyptian language.

TRANSLATION OF THE THIRD DEED (C).

REGISTRY IN GREEK.

In the year XXXV; Pharmuthi [viii] 20. Transacted at the table in Diospolis the Great, at which Lysim[achus] [is president]; in the account of Sarapion and his partners [contractors for the duties] on sales, in which the subscribing clerks are Hermophilus and Sarapion: the purchaser being Pechytes the son of Arsiesis; of the fourth part of an open field of ¿ 3000 square cubits? in the southern part of Diospolis the Great; on the western side of the canal of Her[cules], leading to the river; of which the boundaries are given in the present agreement; which he bought of Ammonius the son of Pyrrhius, and Psenamunis the son of Pyrrhius.   ¿ Pieces 3000?   The end.   Of which . .

Lysimach. has subscribed.

ENCHORIAL AGREEMENT (C).

¿ XXXV ? Month . . In the reign of Ptolemy and Cleopatra his sister, the children of Ptolemy and Cleopatra the Gods Illustrious; and the Priest of Alexander and of the Saviour Gods, of the Brother Gods, of the Beneficent Gods, of the Father loving Gods, of the Illustrious Gods, of the ¿ hostile ? Paternal God, and of the Mother loving Gods and the Prize bearer of Berenice the Beneficent, and the [Gold and Silver] Basket bearer of Arsinoe the Brother loving, and the Priest of Arsinoe the Father loving, being [as appointed in the metropolis]: the bargain was made by the men of the family of Alecis : Ammonius the son of Pyrrhius, and Psenamunis the son of Pyrrhius, coming into the temple . . agreed with Pechytes the son of Arsiesis and ¿ Oenone? to sell for a sum of money . .   (14) Royal Street . . month . . time   . .   Executed and confirmed . Written by . . clerk to the chief priests of Amonrasonther and the contemplar Gods, the Gods ¿ Beneficent ? the Father loving Gods and the Gods Illustrious, the ¿ hostile ? Paternal God, and the Mother loving Gods.   Amen.

The name of Eupator appears here to contain, in two different places, the characters which in the

Rosetta inscription denote hostile or turbulent;
and this circumstance would incline us to prefer
the date of the last year of the reign of Philometor: but it is possible that the same epithets may
have been intended to mean warlike, in a favour-
able sense.

There remains a fourth enchorial manuscript,
of some importance, at present in the British
Museum, but still belonging to Mr. Salt, without
whose permission it would be improper to make
public its whole contents, even if they were perfectly intelligible. But, in fact, the preamble of
this manuscript has been lost, and the registry is
nearly illegible, except that the date is clearly
XLVII, and the signature of the President at the
table of Hermopolis appears to be Dionysius.
The names of Horus and Erieus and Arsiesis
are also distinguishable in the body of the deed,
and the word "two thousand" is written at
length, at the end of the registry. Now the
year 47 can only belong to the reign of Philadelphus, or to that of Eupator, and the style of the
registry too much resembles that of all the other
deeds, including Anastasy's, to allow us to assign
it to the former reign: it must, therefore, belong,
not to 277, but to 124 B. C. This date will not
indeed give us any certain evidence respecting
that of Mr. Grey's deeds; though it might rather
incline us to take the later than the earlier, of two
periods, equally probable in other respects. On

the whole, we can only leave the alternative open for future decision between the dates, as thus contrasted:

Mr. Grey's enchorial deed	(A), **XXVIII**	154 or 143 B.C.	
	(B), **XXIX**	153	142
	(C), **XXXV**	147	136
Mr. Grey's Greek Antigraph, or rather the enchorial deed of Paris	**XXXVI**	146	135
Mr. Salt's enchorial deed	**XLVII**		124
Anastasy's Greek conveyance	**XII-IX**		106.

The registry of Mr. Grey's first deed is therefore at least 37, and, on the whole, most probably 48 years more ancient, than any other writing with a pen and ink that exists; and it still remains in the most perfect preservation. Mr. Jomard has compared the manuscript of Anastasy, for its importance, to the pillar of Rosetta: but it can in no respect whatever be put in competition with the Antigraph of Mr. Grey.

SPECIMEN OF MR. GREY'S ENCHORIAL PAPYRUS.

CHAPTER VI.

EXTRACTS FROM DIODORUS AND HERODOTUS; RE-
LATING TO MUMMIES.

IT is rather as being illustrated by the discovery
of Mr. Grey's Greek papyrus, than as contributing
much to its illustration, that I shall here introduce
such passages of Diodorus Siculus and of Herodotus, as tend to explain the customs of the Egyptians respecting the honours shown to the dead
bodies of their relations.

" The inhabitants of this country," says Diodorus, Book I. § 51, Wess., in the language of Booth,
p. 26, " little value the short time of this present
life; but put a high esteem upon the name and
reputation of a virtuous life after death; and they
call the houses of the living, *Inns*, because they
stay in them but a little while; but the sepulchres of the dead they call *Everlasting habitations*,
because they abide in the graves to infinite generations. Therefore they are not very curious in
the building of their houses; but in beautifying
their sepulchres they leave nothing undone that
[the excess of magnificence can suggest]."

§. 72. W. " What the Egyptians performed, after the deaths of every one of their kings, clearly evidences the great love they bore to them. For honour done to him that cannot possibly know it, in a grateful return of a former benefit, carries along with it a testimony of sincerity, without the least colour of dissimulation." Booth, p. 37.

§ 73. W. The whole of Egypt being divided into a number of parts, called Nomes by the Greeks, each of these is governed by a Nomarcha, to whom the care of all its public concerns is entrusted. The land being every where divided into three portions, the first is occupied by the priesthood, who are held in the greatest respect by the inhabitants, as being devoted to the worship of the gods, and as possessing the greatest power of understanding, from the superiority of their education : and from the revenues of these lands they perform all sacrifices throughout Egypt, and support the servants of the temples as well as their own families : for they hold that the administration of the honours of the gods ought not to be fluctuating, but to be conducted always by the same persons, and in the same manner : and that those, who are above all their fellow citizens in wisdom and knowledge, ought not to be below any of them in the comforts and conveniences of life : and the priests are in the habit of associating very generally with the kings, partly as counsellors, partly as assistants, and partly as ex-

pounders and instructors: foretelling future events
by means of astronomy and of augury, and reading the most useful lessons from the past, out of
the records of their sacred volumes: for it is not
the custom, as in Greece, for one man, or one
woman, to be appointed to each priesthood, but
there are many who are employed together in the
sacrifices and in other ceremonies; and these
transmit the same professional occupation to their
descendants. The whole of the families of the
priests are exempt from taxes, and they come immediately after the king in rank and authority.
The second portion of the land is retained in the
power of the king for his own revenue, out of
which he has to provide for all military expenses,
and for the support of his own splendour and dig-
nity, as well as for the liberal remuneration of
those who have distinguished themselves by their
virtues and their valour: so that being amply
supplied from this territory, they are not obliged
to burden their subjects with oppressive taxes.
The last of the three portions is assigned to the
military population, who are subject to the duties attending on a state of warfare: in order that
those, who are exposed to danger in battle, may
be the more ready to undergo the hazards of the
field, from the interest that they feel in the country as occupiers of the soil: for it would be
thought absurd to commit the common safety to
the care of those, who possessed nothing in the

country that was worthy of preservation: and this system had the still greater advantage of acting as an encouragement to population, in order that the country might not be in want of foreign auxiliaries: and their descendants, in like manner, receiving the constitution thus transmitted to them from their forefathers, are excited by the emulation of the valiant deeds of their ancestors, and become invincible by the courage and experience which they acquire.

§ 74. There are also three other classes that enter into the political system of Egypt; those of the Shepherds, the Husbandmen, and the Artisans. The husbandmen, occupying, at a low rent, the arable land belonging to the king, and the priests, and the military, employ their whole time in cultivating it: and being educated from their infancy in agricultural pursuits, they are superior, from their experience, to the husbandmen of other countries: for they are perfectly well acquainted, partly from the knowledge derived from their ancestors, and partly from their own observation, with the nature of the soil, and its irrigation, and with the times and seasons for sowing and reaping, and for collecting all kinds of fruits. The same advantages are possessed by the shepherds, who receive the charge of the flocks from their forefathers as by inheritance, and pass their whole lives in the care of their cattle: and having derived much information from

their ancestors, respecting the best modes of treat-
ment and fattening of the different animals, they
also add not a little from their own zeal and industry in their occupations: and, what is most
remarkable, from their excessive refinement in
these pursuits, the poulterers and geese feeders,
besides the natural modes of breeding birds, which
are common in other countries, have procured an
infinite multitude of poultry by their own ingenuity : for they do not hatch their eggs by the
incubation of the hens, but, by means of an artificial operation, derived from their own talents and
invention, they are enabled to rival, if not to exceed, the activity of nature: and the arts in general
are carried to a very elaborate degree of perfection
by the Egyptians; for in this country no artist is
allowed to meddle either with political affairs, or
with any other employment, besides that which
he has received from his parents, and to which he
is confined by the law : so that neither the jeal-
ousy of a master, nor any public business, can
ever divert him from the exclusive study of his
profession: for in other countries we often observe
that an artist is diverted by a variety of pursuits,
and is too avaricious to confine himself to his own
work ; some employing themselves in husbandry,
some in commerce, and some in two or three different arts at once; and in democratical countries, many are constantly frequenting popular
assemblies, and doing mischief to the government,

while they are receiving bribes from the leaders
of parties : but among the Egyptians, if any arti-
san should meddle with politics, or should employ himself in any other concerns besides that in
which he has been educated, a severe punishment
would be inflicted on him. Such then were the
institutions of the ancient Egyptians with regard
to their public and private occupations.

§ 75. For the regulation of judicial proceedings, they also took no common pains : since they
held that the sentences, pronounced by the legal
tribunals, had the greatest possible influence, whether beneficial or injurious, on the concerns of
common life : and they saw that the punishment of
offenders, and the relief of oppressed persons,
were the most effectual remedies for the evils of a
state : and that if the terror, that arises from the
condemnation of the guilty, were to be superseded by money or by favour, there would be
nothing but confusion in all ranks of society : and
they attained the end they desired, by the selection of the best men out of the most considerable
cities as Common Judges : taking ten from Heliopolis, and the same number from Thebes and from
Memphis : and the Bench, thus assembled, did not
appear to be inferior either to the Areopagites at
Athens, or to the Elders among the Lacedaemoni-
ns. When these thirty had met, they proceeded to
elect the most distinguished of their number as their
President, with the title of Arch judge : and his

place among themselves was supplied by another person, sent by the same city The judges all received allowances from the king, sufficient for their support, and the arch judge received a manifold portion. He was distinguished by wearing round his neck a golden chain, suspending a figure adorned with precious stones, which was called Alethɪa, or Truth : and the trial began when the arch judge put on this image of Truth. Now the whole of the laws of the country being written in eight books, and these books being placed near the judges, it was the custom for the accuser to write down in detail the offense to be proved, and the manner in which the action was committed, and the estimated amount of the damage or the injury : the accused party then, taking the depositions of his opponents, wrote his answer to each of them, either denying the facts, or maintaining that they were not illegal ; or, if they were illegal, that the damages were appreciated too highly : the accuser replied again in writing, and the accused party rejoined : and both having given in their writings to the judges, the thirty proceeded to declare their opinions among themselves ; and lastly, the arch judge touched one of the contending parties, who was to be successful, with the figure of Truth which he wore .. And this was done, in order to supersede the influence of artificial eloquence, and the fascination of personal appearance, which too often pervert the distribution of justice..

§ 80. The Priests of the Egyptians are allowed
to marry but one wife: other persons marry as
many as they please: but they are obliged to
rear all their children, since a numerous population is esteemed highly conducive to the happiness
of every country and state: and none of their
children are accounted illegitimate, even if the
mother has been purchased as a slave: for the
children are supposed to belong more particularly to the father, the mother being considered
as little more than a nurse. They feed their
children very lightly, and at an incredibly small
expense: giving them a little meal of the coarsest
and cheapest kind, the pith of the papyrus, baked
under the ashes, with the roots and stalks of some
marsh weeds, either raw, or boiled, or roasted:
and since most of them are brought up, on account
of the mildness of the climate, without shoes, and
indeed without any other clothing; the whole of
the expense, incurred by the parents, till they
come to years of maturity, does not exceed about
20 drachmas, or 13 shillings, each. This frugality
is the true reason of the great populousness of
Egypt, and of the magnificence of the public
works, with which the country is adorned.

§ 81. The children of the priests, however,
are instructed in two descriptions of literature;
the sacred and the more general: and they apply
themselves with diligence to geometry and arithmetic: for the river, changing the appearance of
the country very materially every year, is the

cause of many and various discussions among the
neighbouring proprietors : and these it would be
difficult for any person to decide, without geometrical reasoning, founded upon actual observation : and for arithmetic they have frequent occasion both in their domestic economy, and in the
application of geometrical theorems, besides its
utility in the cultivation of astronomical studies :
for the orders and motions of the stars are observed at least as industriously by the Egyptians
as by any other people whatever : and they keep
records of the motions of each for an incredible
number of years ; the study of this science having
been, from the remotest times, an object of national ambition with them : they have also most
punctually observed the motions and periods and
stations of the planets, as well as the powers which
they possess, with respect to the nativities of animals, and what good or evil influences they exert :
and they frequently foretel what is to happen to
a man throughout his life, and not uncommonly
predict a failure of crops, or an abundance, and
the occurrence of epidemic diseases among men
or beasts : they foresee also earthquakes and
floods, and the appearances of comets, and a variety of other things which appear impossible to
the multitude. It is said also that the Chaldaeans
in Babylon are derived from an Egyptian colony,
and have acquired their reputation for astrology
by means of the information obtained from the

priests in Egypt: but the generality of the common people in Egypt learn only, from their parents
or relations, that which is required for the exercise of their peculiar professions, as we have
already seen: a few of them only teach them
something of literature, especially those who cul-
tivate the more refined of the arts: wrestling and
music it is not their custom to practice: for they
conceive that, by exercise in the palaestra, young
men acquire not solid health, but a temporary
increase of strength, which is by no means free
from danger; and music they esteem not only
useless, but even injurious, as rendering the minds
of men effeminate . . .

§. 83. W. The customs of the Egyptians with
regard to their sacred animals are exceedingly
surprising, and worthy to be examined; for they
venerate some of these animals in an extraordinary degree, not only while they are living, but
even after their death: for example, cats, and
ichneumons, and dogs; and besides these, the
hawk and the ibis; furthermore, wolves and cro-
codiles, and other beasts of prey . . Now each
kind of the animals, that are held sacred, has a
piece of ground appropriated to them, affording
a rent sufficient for the care and the food that
they require: the Egyptians are also in the habit
of making vows to some of their divinities on be-
half of their children; and if they recover from
the disease, they shave off their hair, and counter-

poising it with silver or with gold, they give the
money to the priests, who have the care of these
animals: the priests expend this money in articles of food; and cutting up the meat for the
hawks, call out to them with a loud voice, and
throw it to them as they fly near: and for the cats
and the ichneumons they soften the bread in milk,
and lay it before them with the proper calls and
signals ; or give them some of the fishes of the
Nile cut in pieces : and in the same manner they
furnish to every other kind of animal its appropriate food: nor do they attempt to perform these
services with any degree of privacy, or to avoid
the sight of the multitude; but on the contrary
they value themselves, as being the ministers of
the highest honours of the Gods, and travel through
the cities and the country with their appropriate
standards : showing obviously at a distance to
what deities they are attached; and receiving the
universal respect and homage of those who meet
them: and when any one of these animals dies,
they roll it up in fine linen, and bewail themselves,
and beat their breasts, as they carry it to be em-
balmed : and then they embalm it with resins,
and with substances fit to perfume and to preserve it, and bury it in the sacred vaults: and if
any one voluntarily destroys one of these animals,
he suffers death : with the exception of the cat
and the ibis; for if a person kills either of these,
even involuntarily, he infallibly loses his life, a

H

multitude immediately collecting and tearing him
in pieces, often without any form of trial; so
that, for fear of such a calamity, if any one finds
one of these animals dead, he stands at a distance,
and calls out with a loud voice, lamenting, and
protesting that the animal has been found dead.
This superstitious regard to the sacred animals is
so thoroughly rooted in their minds, and every one
of them has his passions so strongly bent upon
their honour, that at the time when Ptolemy had
not yet been called a king by the Romans, and
the people were using every possible effort to
flatter the Italians, who were visiting the country
as strangers, and studious to avoid every thing
that could excite disputes, or lead to war, on
account of their dread of the consequences; a
Roman having killed a cat, and a crowd being
collected about his residence, neither the magis-
trates, who were sent by the king to appease their
rage, nor the general terror of the Roman name,
were able to save the offender from vengeance,
although he had done it unintentionally: and
this we relate, not from the testimony of others,
but from what we ourselves had an opportunity
of seeing, upon our journey to Egypt.

§. 84. If these things appear to many incredible and almost fabulous, what remains to be told
will be thought still more extraordinary In the
time of a great famine in Egypt, it is related
that many of the inhabitants were compelled by

hunger to devour each other, but that nobody was even accused of having touched the flesh of any of the sacred animals. Indeed whenever a dog has died in a house, the whole of the persons, residing in it, shave their whole bodies, and go into mourning: and what is still more remarkable, if there was either wine or corn, or any other provisions, in the house, in which the animal died, they would not dare to make any use of it whatever : and if they lose these animals, while they are absent upon any military expedition, they carry back their cats and their hawks in sorrow to Egypt: this they will do even if they are themselves in want of the means of returning with convenience. The manner in which they treat their Apis in Memphis, and Mneuis in Heliopolis, and the Goat in Mendes, and the Crocodile in the Lake Moeris, and the Lion that is kept at Leontopolis, with many other things of the same kind, is easily narrated, but not easily credited, except by an eye witness : for all these animals are kept in sacred inclosures, and attended by many of the most respectable persons, who supply them with the most delicate food; fine flour or prepared corn, boiled in milk, and all kinds of cakes mixed with honey, and geese, either boiled or roasted, are continually provided for them; and for those which are carnivorous, various birds are caught, and given to them alive : and their whole establishments are arranged on a very expensive scale, for they are furnished with warm baths, and anointed with the finest ointments, and the choicest perfumes are burned before them: they have also rich carpets and ornamented furniture, and care is taken to provide them with female companions of the greatest beauty, who are also fed in the most luxurious manner: and when they die, they are lamented like favourite children, and are buried not according to the means of their attendants only, but often much more magnificently: for after the death of Alexander, when Ptolemy the son of Lagus had lately become King of Egypt, the Apis at Memphis happened to die of old age; and the person, who had the care of him, not only spent the whole of the allowances, which were very considerable, upon the funeral, but borrowed also fifty talents, or twelve thousand pounds, more of Ptolemy, to defray the expense: and within our own memory it has happened, that the guardians of these animals have spent not less than a hundred talents at their funeral.

§. 85. Besides these ceremonies, there are many other customs at the death of the sacred bull named Apis; for after he has been splendidly interred, the priests seek for a calf who is marked as nearly as possible in the same manner: and having found him, they release the public from their mourning, and the appointed persons carry the calf first to Nilopolis, where they feed

him for forty days; and then embarking him on
board of a yacht with a gilded cabin, they conduct him as a god to the sacred grove of Vulcan,
at Memphis. In these forty days only, he is
allowed to be seen by women, who perform certain evolutions before him, which are probably
more amusing to his attendants than to himself:
and at no other time are women allowed to see
him. The reason of the honours paid to him is
said to be, that at the death of Osiris, his soul
transmigrated into this animal, and that it is continually transferred to his successors, when he
dies: others however inform us, that when Osiris
was killed by Typhon, his limbs were collected by
Isis, and thrown into a wooden cow, covered with
cotton cloths, and that the city was thence called
Busiris. [It seems however that this must have
been a Grecian fiction, for in Egyptian BUSIRIS
must have meant the *tomb* of Osiris, and not the
cow.] For the deification of the other animals, as
well as of their kings, a variety of reasons are assigned [; all as uninteresting as they are absurd;
except the story of a hawk having brought, to the
priest at Thebes, a book of laws and religious ob-
servances, tied up with purple; and that hence
the Hierogrammates, or sacred scribes, were distinguished by a purple sash, and by wearing a
hawk's feather on their heads: that the crocodile
is said to be venerated as the watchman of the
Nile, preventing the predatory excursions, which

would be undertaken, if the thieves could swim across the river in safety; and that the diversity of deities, worshipped in neighbouring parts of the country, is supposed by some to have originated in a political contrivance of the government, to keep the people in subjection, by preventing their too intimate union].

§. 91. The customs of the Egyptians, with regard to their funerals, are not the least wonderful of their peculiar institutions. For when any one dies among them, the whole of his family and all his friends cover their heads with clay, and go about the city lamenting, until the body is buried; partaking neither of baths, nor of wine, nor of any abundant food, nor putting on rich clothing. The funerals are conducted upon three different scales, the most expensive, the moderate, and the humblest: the first costs a talent of silver [£250]; the second twenty minae [£60]; the third is extremely cheap. Now the persons, that undertake this office, are artists, who exercise the profession from generation to generation: and they bring to the friends of the deceased an estimate of the expenses of the funeral, and ask them in what manner they wish that it should be performed. When the agreement is made, the operations are commenced by the proper persons: and first the scribe marks out how the dissection is to be performed, upon the left side of the body; the dissector then cuts it

with a sharp Ethiopian stone, and immediately
betakes himself to flight, and is pursued and
beaten, as if he had committed an inhuman action;
the embalmers, on the contrary, are held in all
honour and respect, associating with the priests,
and having free access to the temples, as sacred
persons : these embalmers commence their office
by removing such parts as are most susceptible
of decay, and, washing the rest with palm wine,
and spices, apply various kinds of resins for
more than thirty days, and then impregnate the
whole with myrrh and cinnamon, and other substances calculated not only to preserve it, but to
communicate to it an agreeable smell : and finally
they return the body to the relations, so perfectly
preserved in every part, that even the hairs of the
eyelids and eyebrows remain undisturbed, and
the whole appearance of the person is unchanged,
and the features are capable of being recognised :
so that the Egyptians, very commonly, keeping
the bodies of their ancestors in magnificent apart-
ments, are able to see the very faces of those, who
have died several generations before them : each
of whom being distinguishable, not only by his
height, and the outline of his figure, but even by
the character of his countenance, they enjoy a
wonderful gratification, as if they lived in the
society of those whom they see before them. [It is
indeed related by Damascenus, Orat. i, that they
placed them on seats at their tables, as if they

wished to eat and drink in their society : and
Lucian, in his Essay on Grief, declares, that he
has been an eye witness of the custom. Wessel.
It is not however probable that such a practice
should have been continued in the times of the
Ptolemies: although Lucian, who had an appointment in Egypt under Marcus Aurelius, may be
considered as pretty good authority, when he
speaks seriously.]

§. 92. But when the body is about to be
finally buried, the relations announce the appointed day to the judges, and to all the friends
of the deceased, declaring that he is about to pass.
the lake of the Nome : and forty two judges being
collected, and placed in a semicircle, which is
prepared beyond the lake, a boat is brought up,
which had been provided for the purpose, conducted by a boatman who is called, in their
language, Charon, [the Silent] : whence they
say that Orpheus, in former times, having
travelled into Egypt, and seen this custom, in-
vented the fable of Hades, partly from imitating
what he saw, and partly from his own imagination : but when the boat was brought into the
lake, before the coffin with the dead body was
put on board, it was lawful, for any person who
thought proper, to bring forwards his accusation
against the deceased : and if he showed that the
deceased had led an evil life, the judges declared
accordingly, and the body was deprived of the

accustomed sepulture: but if the accuser failed of establishing what he advanced, he was subject to very heavy penalties. When there had been no accuser, or when the accusation had been repelled as unjust, the relations, laying aside their mourning, pronounced encomiums on the deceased: not enlarging upon his descent, as is usual among the Greeks, for they hold that all the Egyptians are equally noble: but relating his earliest education and the course of his studies, and then his piety and justice in manhood, and his temperance, and the other virtues that he possessed, they supplicated the infernal deities to receive him as a companion of the pious: the multitude in the mean time applauded, and joined in extolling the glory of the deceased, as being about to remain to eternity with the virtuous in the regions of Hades. The body is then placed, by those who have family catacombs already prepared, in the compartment allotted to it: those who are not possessed of catacombs construct a new apartment for the purpose, in their own houses, and set the coffin upright against the firmest of the walls. Those who are debarred of the rites of burial, on account of the accusation which has been brought forwards against them, or on account of debts which they have contracted, are placed in their own houses : and then, if their children's children happen to be prosperous, they are frequently released from the impediments of their creditors and their accusers, and at length obtain the ceremony of a magnificent funeral.

§. 93. It is most solemnly established in Egypt, to pay a more marked respect to their parents and their ancestors, when they are removed to their everlasting habitations. It is also usual among them to deposit the bodies of their deceased parents, as pledges for the payment of money that they borrow: and those who do not redeem these pledges are subject to the heaviest disgrace, and are deprived of burial after their death...

§. 96. We must now enumerate such of the Greeks as have visited Egypt in ancient times, for the acquirement of knowledge and wisdom. The priests of the Egyptians relate, from the records preserved in their sacred volumes, that they were visited by Orpheus and Musaeus, and Melampus and Daedalus; by Homer, the poet, and Lycurgus, the Spartan: by Solon, the Athenian, and Plato, the philosopher: and that Pythagoras, of Samos, also came there, and the mathematician Eudoxus: and Democritus of Abdera, and Oenopides of Chius. All these they identify by some distinct marks, either portraits, or appellations derived from their residences or their works: and they produce evidence from the branches of knowledge, which they respectively cultivated, that they had only borrowed, from the Egyptians, all that acquired them the

admiration of their countrymen. That Orpheus
had learned of them the greatest part of his mystical ceremonies, and the orgies that celebrate
the wanderings [of Ceres], and the mythology of
the shades below : for that the rites of Osiris and
of Bacchus are the same : and those of Isis extremely resemble those of Ceres, with the change
of name only : and the punishments of the impious
in Tartarus, and the Elysian plains of the virtuous,
and the common imagery of fiction, were all copied
from the ceremonies of the Egyptian funerals :
that Hermes, the conductor of souls, was, according
to the old institution of Egypt, to convey the body
of Apis to an appointed place, where it was received by a man wearing the mask of Cerberus,
[probably the *Cteristes* of the temporary nomen-
clature ;] and that Orpheus having related this
among the Greeks, the fable was adopted by
Homer, who makes the Cyllenian Hermes call
forth the souls of the suitors, holding his staff in
his hand :

Cyllenius now to Pluto's dreary reign
Conveys the dead, a lamentable train!
The golden wand that causes sleep to fly,
Or in soft slumber seals the wakeful eye,
That drives the ghosts to realms of night or day,
Points out the long, uncomfortable way.
Trembling the spectres glide, and plaintive vent
Thin, hollow screams, along the deep descent. .

And now they reached the Earth's remotest ends,
And now the gates where evening Sol descends,
And Leucas' rock, and Ocean's utmost streams,
And now pervade the dusky land of dreams;
And rest at last where souls unbodied dwell
In ever flowery meads of Asphodel,
The empty forms of men inhabit there,
Impassive semblance, images of air!

                                        POPE.

The river he calls Ocean, as they say, because
the Egyptians call the Nile Oceanus in their
own language [? ?]: the gates of the Sun
are derived from Heliopolis: and the meadow
is so called, from the lake which is named
Acherusian, and which is near Memphis, being
surrounded by beautiful meadows, and canals,
with lotus and flowering rushes: and that
it is consistent with the imitation to make
the deceased inhabit these places: because the
greater number and the most considerable of
the Egyptian catacombs are there, the bodies
being ferried over the river and the Acherusian
lake, and the mummies being deposited in the
catacombs there situated. And the rest of the
Grecian mythology respecting Hades agrees
also with the present practice in Egypt: the
boat which carries over the bodies, and is called
BARIS; and the penny that is given for the fare
to the boatman, who is called CHARON in the

language of the country. They say there is
also, in the neighbourhood of the same place,
a temple of the nocturnal Hecate, with the gates
of Cocytus and of Lethe, fastened with brazen
bars; and that there are, besides, other gates of
Truth; and near them a figure of Justice without
a head.

§. 97. In the city of Acanthae, on the Libyan
side of the Nile, 120 stadia from Memphis, they
say there is a barrel pierced with holes, to
which 360 of the priests carry water from the
Nile : and that a mystery is acted in an assembly
in that neighbourhood, in which a man is made
to twist one end of a long rope, while other
persons untwist the other end; an allusion to
which has become proverbial in Greece.   Melampus, they say, brought from Egypt the mysteries
of Bacchus, and the stories of Saturn, and the
battles of the Titans: and Daedalus imitated
the Egyptian labyrinth, in that which he built
for king Minos: the Egyptian labyrinth having
been constructed by Mendes, or by Marus,
an ancient king, many years before his time;
and that the style of the ancient statues in
Egypt is the same with that of the statues
sculptured in Greece : but that the very fine
Propylon of Vulcan in Memphis was the work
of Daedalus as an architect : and that being
admired for this work, he had the honour of
obtaining a place, in the same temple, for a

wooden statue of himself, which was the work
of his own hands : that his talents and inventive
faculties at last acquired him even divine
honours, and that there is to this day a temple
of Daedalus, on one of the islands near Memphis,
which is honoured by the neighbouring inhabitants. That Homer had been in Egypt, they
argue, among other reasons, from the administration of the Nepenthes by Helen to Telemachus,
which occasioned a forgetfulness of the evils
that had befallen him : for he seems to have
perfectly understood the nature of this remedy,
which he says Helen received in the Egyptian
Thebes, of Polydamne the wife of Thon, for
that the women of the same place still make
use of it, for a similar purpose, and it is only
among the Diospolitan women, that it is known
as a remedy for anger and for sorrow, and that
Diospolis is the Thebes of the ancients ; and
that Venus is called golden by its inhabitants
from an old tradition, and that there is a field
belonging to the golden Venus in the neighbourhood of Momemphis : and that he has copied
from them the history of the embraces of Jupiter
and Juno, and of Jove's absence in Ethiopia :
for that they have an annual ceremony, in which
the temple or shrine of Jupiter is carried across
the river into Libya, and is brought back in
a few days, as if the deity returned from Ethiopia:
and that the embraces of the deities are found

(§. 346) in their assemblies, when both of their
shrines are carried to a mountain which is
strewed by the priest with flowers. [Analogies
all too slight to be admitted as any thing like
evidence.]

§. 98. They say also that Lycurgus and
Plato and Solon transferred many of the customs of the Egyptians into their own establishments. And that Pythagoras learned in Egypt
both his divinity and his geometrical theorems,
and his arithmetic, and the transmigration of
the soul into all kinds of animals. They believe
too that Democritus spent five years among them,
and was taught by them many things relating
to astronomy. And that Oenopides [of Chius]
in the same way, by living with their priests and
astronomers, learned of them, among many
other things, the position of the sun's orbit, that
it moved obliquely, and in a direction contrary
to that of the other stars. And that Eudoxus,
in the same manner, gained great reputation
among his countrymen, by having studied astronomy among them, and made known many of their
useful discoveries among the Greeks : and the
most celebrated of the ancient statuaries had
lived among them, Telecles and Theodorus, the
sons of Rhoecus, who made for the Samians
the image of the Pythian Apollo : for it is said
that one half of the image was executed in Samos
by Telecles, and the other half at Ephesus by his

brother Theodorus; and that both parts, when put together, agreed so well with each other, as to appear precisely as if they had been the work of one person : and that this kind of workmanship was never practised by the Greeks, but was very common among the Egyptians: for that with them it was not usual to judge of the symmetry of a figure by the sight of the whole, as with the Greeks; but that when the stones were quarried and properly cut out, they then proceeded by proportion from the smallest to the greatest; and dividing the whole fabric of the body into one and twenty parts, and a quarter, they arranged the whole symmetry accordingly : and hence, when their artists consult with each other about the magnitude of any figure, although separated from each other, they still make the results agree so well, that this peculiarity of their practice excites the greatest astonishment : and that the image in Samos, according to this refinement of the Egyptians, being divided from the summit of the head, and as far as the middle, is still perfectly consistent with itself, and in all parts alike: they also observe that it extremely resembles the Egyptian figures as having the hands stretched out, and the legs separated, as in walking.   And enough has now been said of what is most celebrated and remarkable in the country and customs of the Egyptians : [the greater part of which is of much more value, as occasionally furnishing anecdotes from the arguments that were advanced by the priests in there discussions, than as by any means rendered fully credible by the application of these anecdotes.]

The process of embalming is described very nearly in the same manner by Herodotus. " Their customs," he says, Book II. § 85, " relating to mourning and to funerals are these. When any person of consequence dies, the females of his family cover their heads and faces with clay, and leaving the dead body at home, wander through the city, beating themselves, wearing a close girdle, and having their bosoms bare, accompanied by all their intimate friends : the men also make similar lamentations in a separate company : they then proceed to embalm the body.

(86). This service is performed by persons appointed to exercise the art, as their business : and when a dead body is brought to them, they show their patterns of mummies in wood, imitated by sculpture : and the most elaborate of these they say belongs to the character of [Osiris] one, whose name I do not think it pious to mention on such an occasion : the second, that they show, is simpler and less costly : the third, the cheapest of all : and having shown them these, they inquire in which way the service shall be performed : the parties then make their agreement, and the body is left for preparation. The

interior soft parts being removed both from the
head and from the trunk, the cavities are washed
with palm wine and fragrant gums, and partly
filled up with myrrh and cassia and other spices;
the whole is then steeped in a solution of soda
for seventy days, which is the longest time per-
mitted; and then, having been washed, the body
is rolled up with bandages of cotton cloth, being
first smeared with gum, instead of glue. The relations then, receiving the body, procure a wooden
case for it in a human shape, and inclose the dead
body in it: and when thus inclosed, they treasure
it up in an appropriate building or apartment,
placing it upright against the wall. And this is the
most expensive mode of preparation.

(87). For those who prefer the middle class,
in order to avoid expense, the process is simpli-
fied by omitting the actual removal of the interior
parts, and introducing a corrosive liquid to melt
them down: the soda consumes the flesh, so that
skin and bone only is left, when the body is restored to the friends.

(88). The third and simplest process is merely
to cleanse the body well, within and without, by
means of some vegetable decoctions, and to keep
it in the alkaline solution for the seventy days,
without further precautions."

It is difficult to say, according to these state-
ments, what part of the ceremony might be considered as actually constituting the burial. But

we find in a Greek inscription on the coffin of a
mummy, found by Mr. Grey, which he has had
the goodness to communicate to me, "The tomb
of Tphuto (or Tphus) the daughter of Heracleus
Soter and Sarapus. She was born in the Vth
year of Adrian our Lord, the 2d Athyr [III], and
died in the XIth year, Tybi [v] the 10th. Aged
six years, two months, and eight days. She was
buried in the XIIth year, the 12th of Athyr."
So that here the burial took place a full year
after the death; and there was time enough for
every imaginable luxury of the embalmer's art.
The coffin is not, in this instance, made in imitation " of the human form," as the coffins of the
more ancient mummies, but it is merely an oblong
trunk, with an arched cover, and a pillar rising
a little at each angle. We have no precise account
of the liturgies, or services, performed to these
canonized personages, but they were probably
some forms of adoration, combined with offerings
of flowers and fruit, which were placed before or
beside them, and it is well known that some corn
and some cakes have been found still standing in
baskets, in some of the catacombs lately opened;
and that specimens of them have been brought
to the British Museum.

CHAPTER VII.

THE manner in which the Hieroglyphical alphabet was employed, in the time of the Roman
emperors, may be understood from the examination of the specimens inserted in this chapter;
they comprehend an example of each of the names
and titles, which Mr. Champollion has included
in his catalogue. In order to illustrate the vene-
ration paid to the Roman emperors in Egypt, I
shall subjoin an extract from Strabo, relating to
the administration of that country, in the days
of the earlier Caesars, for he was a contemporary
and a subject of Tiberius.

Book XVII. "The whole of Egypt was divided
into Nomes, the Thebaid containing ten, the Delta
ten, and the intermediate parts sixteen, making in
all 36 .. The nomes were generally divided into
Toparchiae, or local governments: and these again
into other portions.. At Alexandria, the Necro-
polis is a separate suburb, containing gardens,
and sepulchres, and subterraneous passages, employed for preserving the dead."

" After the death of Julius Caesar, and after the battle of Philippi, Antony went into Asia, and paid extravagant honours to Cleopatra, even making her his wife, and having several children by her. He carried on, in concert with her, the war that was terminated at Actium, and accompanied her, as is well known, in her flight. Augustus following them, destroyed them both, and set Egypt at rest from the revels of a drunkard. It is now governed as a province, or an Eparchia, paying considerable taxes, but being always administered by moderate men, who are sent as Governors, and who hold the rank of a king. Under the governor is the Dicaeodotes, that is the lawgiver, or chancellor: another officer is called the Privy purse, or private accountant, whose business it is to take charge of every thing which is left without an owner, and which falls of right to the Emperor. These two are also attended by Freedmen and Stewards of Caesar, who are intrusted with affairs of greater or less magnitude. There are also three battalions of soldiers, one in the city of Alexandria, the others in the country. Besides these, there are nine companies of Romans; three in the city, three in garrison at Syene, upon the frontiers of Ethiopia, and three in other parts of the country. There are also three regiments of cavalry, similarly distributed, among the fittest places. But of the natives, who are employed in the government of the different cities, the principal are the Exegetes, or Expounder, who is dressed in purple, and is honoured according to the usages of the country, and takes care of what is necessary for the welfare of the city; and the Register, or writer of commentaries; and the Archidicastes, or chief judge; and fourthly, the Captain of the Night. These same magistracies existed in the time of the kings: but the kings governed so ill, that the welfare of the state was disturbed by all kinds of irregularities. Polybius, who was in Egypt, expresses his horror of the condition of the country at that time: he says there were three kinds of inhabitants in Alexandria; the Egyptians, or the people of the country, a keen and civilised race, and the mercenary troops, who were numerous and turbulent; for it was the custom to keep foreign soldiers in their pay, who, having arms in their hands, were more ready to govern than to obey: the third description of people were the Alexandrians, not very decidedly tractable, for similar reasons, but still, better than the last: for those, who had mixed with them, were originally Greeks, and remembered the habits of their country. This part of the population was however then dwindling away, more especially through Evergetes Physcon, in whose reign Polybius came to Alexandria: for on several occasions, when there had been some seditious proceedings he attacked this plebeian multitude with his troops, and de-

stroyed great numbers of them. Polybius could
not therefore help exclaiming, that he had " To
Egypt come, a long and weary way," with but
little pleasure or comfort. The subsequent sovereigns administered their governments as ill, or
still worse. The Romans may be said to have
effected a great reformation in many respects, and
to have regulated the city very effectually; and
in the country they appointed persons as Com-
manders, and Monarchae, and Ethnarchae, that
is, masters of single places, and of districts, without
very extensive powers . . With respect to the
revenues of the country, we may judge of them
from Cicero, who mentions, in one of his orations,
that Auletes, the father of Cleopatra, had an
income, from the taxes, of twelve thousand five
hundred talents, [between three and four millions
sterling]. If then a king, who administered his
government in the worst and most negligent
manner possible, received so large a revenue,
what are we to suppose it must be at present,
when it is managed with so much care, and when
it has been so much increased by the enlargement
of the Indian and African commerce ? In former
times, there were not twenty vessels, that ventured
to navigate the Red Sea, so as to pass out of the
Straights : but now there are great fleets, that
make the voyage to India, and to the remotest
parts of Ethiopia, returning, laden with very valuable cargos, to Egypt, whence they are distri-

buted to other parts; so that they are subjected
to a double duty, first upon importation, and then
upon exportation: and the customs upon these
valuable articles are themselves proportionally
valuable; besides that they have the advantages
of a monopoly : since Alexandria alone is so situated, as to afford, in general, the only warehouse
for receiving them, and for supplying other places
with them."

From a comparison of the Enchorial names,
which are here inserted, we may confidently add
to the alphabet a semicircle, open above, as a
form of the P; we have also several variations of
the T, and perhaps of the TH; and the character,
which is sometimes represented by z, and sometimes by s, must, in all probability, be the Coptic
SH; so that ZMINIS ought rather to be written
SHMINIS, meaning OCTAVIUS, from SHMEN, *eight*.
The same character is found in the phrase of the
Pillar of Rosetta, "who has *received* the kingdom
from his father;" and may probably have belonged
to the word SHEP, if it is allowable to pursue the
analogy so far: it is also remarkable, that the
hieroglyphic, which corresponds to this character,
has very nearly the same form with that, to which
Mr. Champollion attributes the power of SH or X
in the name of Xerxes. His Enchorial form of
the CH is wholly unsupported by any of these
names.

ALPHABET OF CHAMPOLLION.

A

B *

K, Γ

T, Δ *

E

I, H *

Λ *

M *

N *

Ω, O *

Φ, Π *

P

Σ *

TO

*Y: †B.

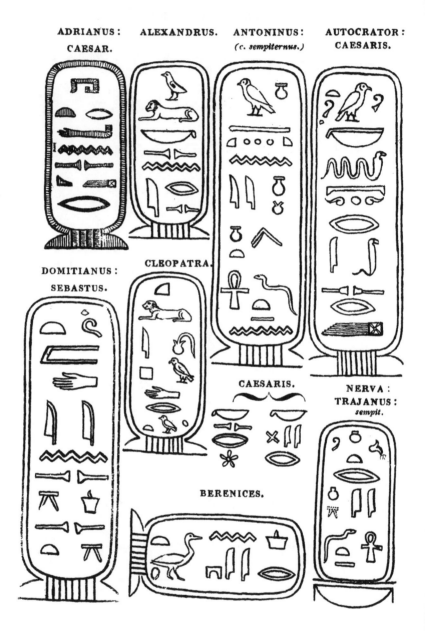

ADRIANUS: ALEXANDRUS. ANTONINUS: AUTOCRATOR:
CAESAR.   *(c. sempiternus.)* CAESARIS.

DOMITIANUS: CLEOPATRA.
SEBASTUS.

CAESARIS.

NERVA:
TRAJANUS:
sempit.

BERENICES.

PTOLEMAEUS :
c. **NEOCAESARIS :**
semp : dil : Is : Phth.

SABINA.

SEBASTE :
sempiterna.

SEBASTUS :
semp. Is : Fhth.

TRAJANUS :
CAESARIS : *semp.*

TRAJANUS : C.
GERMANICUS : .
DACICUS.

VESPASIANUS :
PIUS ?

TIBERIUS :
CAESARIS : *semp*

COGNOMINE.

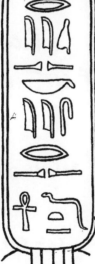

AËTUS

ALECIS, LECIS?

ALEXANDER ⎫

ALEXANDRIA ⎭

AMENOTHES

AMMON, JUPITER

AMMONIUS

AMONORYTIUS

AMONRASONTHER

ANTIGENES

ANTIMACHUS

APOLLONIUS

AREIA

ARM"ENIS"

ARSIESIS

ARSINOE

ASUS, ASYS, ASOS

ATHYR

BERENICE

BUSIRITES

CHAPOCHONSIS

CHAPOCRATES

CHIMNARAUS

CLEOPATRA

DIOGENES

EIRENE, IRENE

ERIEUS

HORUS

ISIS

LUBAIS

LYCOPOLIS

Maësis

Mechir

Mesore

Mirsis

Muthes

Nechthmonthes

Onnophris

Osiris

Osoroeris

Pacemis

Panas

Pateutemis }   {

Peteutemis

Pechýtes

Petearpocrates

Peteartres

PETECHONSIS	
PETEMESTUS	
PETENEPHOTES	
PETEURIS	
PETOPHOIS	
PETOSIRIS	
PHABIS	
PHANRES	
PHIBIS	
PHILINUS	
PORTIS	
PSENAMUNIS	
PSENCHONSIS	
PTOLE- ⎱ MAEUS ⎰	
PYRRHA	
PYRRHIUS	

SENERIEUS	
SENOSOR	
SENPOERIS	
SNACHOMES	
SNACHOMNEUS	
SOTER	
SPOTUS	
TBAEAIS	
TEEPHBIS	
THOTH, HERMES	
THOYTH	
THYNABUNUN	
TOTOES	
ZMINIS	
ZTHENAËTES	
ZOGLYPHUS	

From these specimens, we are also enabled
to make some further inferences respecting the
" popular" system of writing among the Egyptians. They show incontestably, that the employment of the alphabet, discovered by Akerblad,
is not altogether confined to foreign, or at least
to Grecian names : it is applicable, for example,
very readily, to the words Lubais, Tbaeais, Phabis,
and perhaps to some others. But they exhibit
also unequivocal traces of a kind of syllabic
writing, in which the names of some of the deities
seem to have been principally employed, in order
to compose that of the individual concerned : thus
it appears, that wherever both M and N occur,
either together, or separated by a vowel, the
symbol of the god Ammon or Amun is almost
uniformly employed : for example in AMENO-
thes, AMONorytius, AMONrasonther, ChiMNaraus,
PsenAMUNis, and SnachoMNeus, in which we
find neither M nor N, but the symbol for AMMON,
or Jupiter. It follows therefore, that such must
have been the original pronunciation of the word,
and that this deity was not called either HO or
NO, as Akerblad was disposed to imagine. In
the same manner we have traces of Osiris, Arueris,
Isis, and Re ; in *Osoroeris*, *Petosiris*, *Senpoeris*,
Arsiesis, *Maesis*, and *Peteartres*. The SE, in PSEnamunis and SEnerieus, is the symbol for a child,
and is probably a contraction of SHERI : the gender
seems to be distinguished in the enchorial name,
while the distinction is lost in the alphabetical
mode of writing.

K

CHAPTER VIII.

CHRONOLOGICAL HISTORY OF THE PTOLEMIES,
EXTRACTED FROM VARIOUS AUTHORS.

i. *EXTRACT from* Porphyry, *an author of the age of Diocletian, as quoted in Scaliger's* Eusebius, *and probably* thence *in the Armenian translation.*

Alexander, the Macedonian, died in the CXIVth Olympiad, after a reign of 12 years in the whole: and was succeeded in his kingdom by Aridaeus, whose name was changed to Philip, being brother to Alexander, by another mother; for he was the son of Philip by Philinna of Larissa: and after a reign of seven years, he was killed in Macedonia, by Polysperchon the son of Antipater.

Now Ptolemy the son of Arsinoe and of Lagus, after one year of this reign, by an appointment derived from Philip, was sent as a Satrap into Egypt; which he governed in this capacity for 17 years, and afterwards, with Royal authority, for 23; so that the number of all the years of his government, to the time of his death, became 40; but since he retired from the government two years before, in favour of his son Ptolemy Philadelphus, and considered himself as a subject of his son, who had been crowned in his place, the years of this first Ptolemy, called Soter, are reckoned not 40, but 38 only.

He was succeeded by his son, surnamed, as

already mentioned, Philadelphus, who reigned
two years during his fathers' life, and thirty [six]
afterwards, so that his whole reign occupied, like
his father's, 38 years.

In the third place, the throne was ascended
by Ptolemy surnamed Evergetes, who reigned 25
years.

In the fourth by Ptolemy called Philopator,
whose reign was in the whole 17 years.

After him, the fifth Ptolemy was surnamed
Epiphanes, and reigned 24 years.

Epiphanes had two sons, both named Ptolemy,
who reigned after him; the elder was surnamed Philometor, and the younger Evergetes the second ;
their reigns together occupy a period of 64 years.
We have placed this as a single number, because,
as they were at variance with each other, and
reigned alternately, the dates were necessarily
confounded.   For Philometor first reigned eleven
years alone ; but when Antiochus made war upon
Egypt, and deprived him of his crown, the Alexandrians committed the government to the charge
of his younger brother ; and, having driven back
Antiochus, set Philometor at liberty.   They then
numbered the year the [twelfth] of Philometor
and the first of Evergetes ; and this system was
continued till the seventeenth: but from the
eighteenth forwards, the years are attributed to
Philometor alone.

For the elder, having been expelled from his
kingdom by the younger, was restored by the

Romans; and he retained the crown of Egypt, leaving his brother the dominion of Libya, and continued to reign alone for 18 years. He died in Syria, having conquered that country: Evergetes being then recalled from Cyrene, and proclaimed King, continued to number the years of his reign from his first accession to the crown; so that having reigned [29] years after the death of his brother, he extended his dates to 54: for the 36th year of Philometor, which should have been called his 1st, he determined to make the 25th. In the whole therefore we have 64: first 35 of Philometor, and the remainder of Evergetes: but the subdivision may lead to confusion.

Now Ptolemy Evergetes the second had two sons, called Ptolemy, by Cleopatra; the elder Soter, and the younger [Alexander]. The elder was proclaimed king by his mother: and appearing to be obsequious to her wishes, he was beloved for a certain time: but when, in the tenth year of his reign, he put to death the friends of his parents, he was deposed by his mother for his cruelty, and driven as a fugitive into Cyprus.

The mother then sent for her younger son from Pelusium, and proclaimed him sovereign together with herself; so that they reigned in common, the dates of public acts being referred to both: and the year was called the eleventh of Cleopatra, and the eighth of Ptolemy Alexander: comprehending the time as a part of his reign, which began with the fourth year of his brother; during

which he reigned in Cyprus: and this custom
continued during the whole of the life of Cleopatra: but after her death the epoch of Alexander
alone was employed; and, though he actually
held the sceptre for eighteen years only, from the
time of his return to Alexandria, he appears, in
his public records, as having reigned twenty six.
In his nineteenth year, having quarrelled with his
troops, he went out into the country in order to
raise a force to control them; but they pursuing
him, under the command of Tyrrhus, a relation
of the royal family, engaged him by sea, and
compelled him to fly, with his wife and daughter,
to Myrae, a city of Lycia: whence crossing over
to Cyprus, and being attacked by Chaereas, who
had the command of the hostile fleet, he was killed
in battle.

The Alexandrians, after his flight, sent an em-
bassy to the elder Ptolemy, Soter [or Lathurus],
inviting him back from Cyprus, to take possession
of the kingdom. During the seven years and six
months that he survived, after his return, the
whole time that had elapsed since the death of his
father was attributed to his reign: so that the number of years became 35, and six months, of which,
however, only 17 and six months properly belonged
to him, in the two separate portions of his reign:
while the second brother, Alexander, had reigned
18 in the intermediate time: and although
these could not be effaced from the annals, they
suppressed them as far as it was in their power;

since he had offended them by some alliance with
the Jews. They do not therefore reckon these
years separately, but attribute the whole 36 to
the elder brother, omitting again to assign to
Cleopatra, the daughter of the elder, and wife of
the younger brother, who took possession of the
government after her father's death, the six months
that she reigned, which were a part of the 36th
year. Nor did they distinguish by the name of
the Alexander, that succeeded her, the nineteen
days that he retained the crown.

This Alexander was the son of the younger
brother, Ptolemy Alexander, and the step son of
Cleopatra; he was residing at Rome, and the
Egyptian dynasty failing of male heirs, he came
by invitation to Alexandria, and married this
same Cleopatra [his step mother]; and having
deprived her by force of her authority, he put
her to death after 19 days, and was himself killed
in the Gymnasium, by the guards, whom his bar-
barity had disgusted.

Alexander the second was succeeded by
Ptolemy, who was called Neus Dionysus, or the
young Bacchus, the son of Ptolemy Soter, and
the brother of the Cleopatra last mentioned: his
reign continued for 29 years.

His daughter Cleopatra was the last of the
family of the Lagidae, and the years assigned to
her reign are 22.

Neither did these different reigns fill up the
whole series of years from beginning to end in a

regular order, but several of them were intermixed with the others. For, in the time of Dionysus, three years are attributed to his two daughters, Cleopatra Tryphaena,, and Berenice; a year conjointly, and two years, after the death of Cleopatra Tryphaena, to Berenice alone; because in this interval Ptolemy was gone to Rome, and was spending his time there, while his daughters, as if he were not about to return, took possession of the government for themselves; Berenice having also called in to a share of her dominion some men who were her relations: until Ptolemy, returning from Rome, and forgetting the indulgence due to a daughter, took offence at her conduct, and deprived her of life.

The first years of the reign of his successor Cleopatra were also referred to her in common with her elder brother Ptolemy; and the following to other persons, for this reason: Ptolemy Neus Dionysus, [or Auletes], left at his death four children, two Ptolemies, and Cleopatra, and Arsinoe; appointing as his successors his two elder children, Ptolemy and Cleopatra; they were considered as joint sovereigns for four years, and would have remained so; but that Ptolemy, having departed from his father's commands, and resolved to keep the whole power in his own hands, it was his fate to be slain in a sea fight near the coasts of Egypt, by Julius Caesar, who took part with Cleopatra.

After the destruction of this Ptolemy, Cleopatra's younger brother, also named Ptolemy, was placed on the throne with his sister, by Caesar's decree, and the year was called the fifth of Cleopatra, and the first of Ptolemy : and this custom continued till his death, for two more years. But when he had been destroyed by the arts of Cleopatra, in his fourth year and in the eighth of his sister, the subsequent years were distinguished by the name of Cleopatra alone, as far as fifteen. The sixteenth was named also the first, since, after the death of Lysimachus, king of Chalcis in Syria, the "Autocrator" Marc Antony gave Chalcis and all the neighbouring country to Cleopatra ; and from this time the remaining years of her reign, as far as the 22nd, which was the last, were reckoned in the same manner, with an additional number, the 22nd having been called also the 7th, [as the Armenian has very properly read, for the 27th].

From Cleopatra the government devolved to Octavius Caesar, called also Augustus, who overcame the power of Egypt in the battle of Actium, the second year of the CLXXXIVth Olympiad. And from the first year of the CXIth Olympiad, when Aridaeus Philippus [or rather Alexander], the son of Philip, took possession of the government, to the second of the CLXXXIVth, there are 73 Olympiads and a year, or 293 years. And so many are the years of the sovereigns that reigned in Alexandria, to the time of the death of Cleopatra.

ii. *Blair's Chronology of the Ptolemies.*

Year of Nab.	Olympiad.		B. C.		
413	CXI, year	1	336		Aug. Alexander succeeds Philip.
426	CXIV,	2	323		Apr. 21 ; Alexander dies : Ptolemy S. 1.
464	CXXIII,	4	285	39	Ptolemy Soter.
465	CXXIV,	1	284	1	Ptolemy Philadelphus.
502	CXXXIII,	2	247	38	
503		3	246	1	Ptolemy Evergetes.
527	CXXXIX,	3	222	25	
528		4	221	1	Ptolemy Philopator.
544	CXLIII,	4	205	17	
545	CXLIV,	1	204	1	Ptolemy Epiphanes.
568	CXLIX,	4	181	24	
569	CL,	1	180	1	Ptolemy Philometor.
579	CLII,	3	170	11	
580		4	169	12	Ptolemy [Eupator.]
600	CLVII,	4	149	35	Ptolemy Philometor.
604	CLVIII,	4	145	1	Ptolemy [Eupator.]
632	CLXV,	4	117	21	
633	CLXVI,	1	116	9	Ptolemy Lathurus and Cleopatra.
642	CLXVIII,	2	107	10	
643		2	106	1	Cleopatra and Alexander.
660	CLXXII,	4	89	18	
661	CLXXIII,	1	88	1	Ptolemy Lathurus.
667	CLXXIV,	3	82	7	
668		4	81	[1]	Cleopatra II, 6 months: Alexander II, 19 days.
669	CLXXV,	1	80	1	Ptolemy Alexander III.
683	CLXXVIII,	3	66	15	
684		4	65	1	Ptolemy Auletes.
697	CLXXXII,	1	52	14	
698		2	51	1	Ptolemy Dionysius II, and Cleopatra III.
702	CLXXXIII,	2	47	5	
703		3	46	1	Cleopatra III, Ptolemy, jun.
704		4	45	2	
705	CLXXXIV,	1	44	3	Ptolemy dies, leaving Cleopatra III.
719	CLXXXVII,	3	30	17	Sept. 2. Battle of Actium. Augustus makes Egypt a Roman Province.

iii. *Chronology of the Ptolemies, according to Champollion Figeac.* Annales des Lagides, 2 v. 8. Par. 1819.

B. C.

323 May 30, Death of Alexander, Nab. 424 Ol. CXIII, 4.
323 Oct.   Ptolemy Soter arrives in Egypt.
285 End. 39 Ptolemy places Philadelphus on the throne.
284 Nov. 2 1 Philadelphus.
246 Sum. 38 : 1 of Evergetes.
221 Sum.   25 : 1 of Philopator.
204 March 29, 17 : 1 of Epiphanes.
180 March   24 : 1 of Philometor.
146 Aut. 35 : 1 of Evergetes II. [Eupator.]
117 Oct. 29 : 1 of Lathurus.
107 Sum. 10 Lathurus expelled; Alexander reigns.
88 Sum.   29 Lathurus restored; Alexander dies.
81 Middle 36: 1 Lathurus dies Berenice reigns 6 mouths :
             Alexander II.
72 Beg.   8 : 1 Ptolemy Auletes, "22 years" only.
51 Spr. "22": 1 Cleopatra with her brother Ptolemy.
47 July   5 of Cleopatra : 1 of Ptolemy the younger.
44 July   8 Ptolemy poisoned early in the year.
41 July   11 Caesarion takes the title of king; [the Neo-
             caesar of the Hieroglyphical alphabet.]
30 Sept. 2 22 Battle of Actium.
29 Aug. 1 22 Cleopatra kills herself. Egypt a Roman
             Province.

iv. *Mr. St. Martin's Chronology of the Ptolemies.* Recherches sur la Mort d'Alexandre, 8 Par. 1820.

Nabon. B. C.
424 324 June 22 Death of Alexander Ol. CXIII, 4.
     323 Nov. 8 Ptolemy Soter governor of Egypt,
                17 years.
     306 Nov. 1 Ptolemy Soter king; reigns 21 years.
     285 Nov. 7 Soter and his son Philadelphus reign,
                2 years.
     283 Oct. 17 Philadelphus ; reigns alone 36 years.
     247 Nov. 8 Ptolemy Evergetes; reigns 25 years.
     222 Nov. 2 Ptolemy Philopator; reigns 17 years.

" 210 Oct. 9 Ptolemy Epiphanes associated in the crown."

" 208 Oct. 28 First year named after Epiphanes with his father."

205 Oct. 13 Epiphanes reigns alone, 24 years

199 March 28 Anticipated coronation of Epiphanes.

181 Oct. 28 Ptolemy Philometor reigns alone 11 years.

170 Oct. 29 With Evergetes II. [Eupator] 6 years.

164 Oct. 21 Alone again, 18 years ; Evergetes at Cyrene.

146 Nov. 2 Evergetes II. alone 29 years.

117 Nov. 10 Soter II. [Lathurus] with Cleopatra 10 years.

114 Nov. 8 Alexander I. reigns 7 years in Cyprus.

107 Oct. 21 Alexander reigns 18 years : Soter in Cyprus

89 Nov. 1 Soter II. restored, reigns 8 years.

82 Oct. 17 Last of Soter : Berenice reigns 6 months ; Alexander II. 19 days.

81 Nov. 4 Ptolemy Auletes ; reigns 29 years.

59 Feb. 24 In the Roman year beginning this day, Auletes was acknowledged king by the Senate.

58 Feb. 14 He was driven out of Egypt after this day, which was the beginning of a Roman year.

58 Oct. 21 Cleopatra Tryphaena and Berenice ; 1 year.

57 Nov. 7 Berenice ; 2 years with Cybiosactes and Archelaus.

55 May 2 Auletes had been re-established.

52 Nov. 12 Cleopatra with the elder Ptolemy ; 4 years.

48 June 29 Battle of Pharsalia.

47 Feb. 6 Alexandria taken by Caesar ; death of Ptolemy.

47 Oct. 18 Cleopatra with the younger Ptolemy.

44 Oct. 15 Cleopatra alone ; 14 years.

31 Sept. 2 Battle of Actium.

Oct. 21 Last year of Cleopatra begins.

30 Aug. 1 Alexandria taken by Augustus : end of the Lagidae.

Mr. St. Martin being the latest chronologist, that has examined these dates, I have thought it right to insert his table, which I suppose to be correct in the principal part of its foundation, although I cannot readily believe that he is right in attributing to the Ptolemies the observance of the Macedonian year rather than of the Egyptian. He says that in Egypt, as all the world knows, the years of the sovereigns were reckoned from the first day of the year, in which they took the reins of government: meaning by this the first day of the Macedonian year : it appears, however, unquestionable from almost every inscription and manuscript found in Egypt, which exhibits a date, that the Egyptian months and years were employed almost exclusively in that country   It happens, however, that about the time in question, the beginning of these years did not vary very exorbitantly from each other: the Egyptian year having begun in September, October, November or December: and the Macedonian, according to Mr. St. Martin, in October or November.

v. *Genealogy of the Ptolemies, from Champollion Figeac I, p.* 231.

Reigns.	Names and Descriptions.	Reigned.	Death.	Wives.	Children.
I.	SOTER. Son of Lagus and Arsinoe, first governor, then King.	39 y. 5 m.	Natural.	1. 2. 3. Eurydice, d. of Antipater. 4. Berenice died old.	[Arsinoe.] Ceraunus: seized the crown of Macedonia. Philadelphus: succeeded him.
II.	PHILADELPHUS. Son of Soter and Berenice.	37 y. 11 m.	Natural.	1. Arsinoe d. of Lysimachus, and of his sister. 2. Arsinoe, her mother.	Evergetes. None.
III.	EVERGETES: Tryphon; son of Philadelphus and Arsinoe.	25 y.	Poisoned by his son.	Berenice, daughter of Magas.	Philopator. Magas: put to death by his brother. Arsinoe.
IV.	PHILOPATOR: Gallus; son of Evergetes and Berenice.	16 y. 5 m.	Natural.	Arsinoe his sister: killed by her husband.	Epiphanes.
V.	EPIPHANES. Son of Philopator and Arsinoe.	24 y.	Poisoned.	Cleopatra, d. of the king of Syria, survived him 8 y.	Philometor. Cacergetes. Cleopatra.
VI.	PHILOMETOR. Son of Epiphanes and Cleopatra.	11 y.			
VII.	EVERGETES II: Physcon Cacergetes. Philologus. [Eupator.] Brother of Philometor.	4 y.			
VIII.	PHILOMETOR and EVERGETES.	2 y.			
IX.	PHILOMETOR.	18 y.	Fall from his horse.	Cleopatra his sister.	A son: killed by his uncle. Cleop. Cocce.
X.	EVERGETES II.	29 y.	Natural.	1. Cleopatra, his brother's widow, repudiated. 2. Cleopatra Cocce, her daughter.	Memphites killed by his father. Lathurus. Alexander Tryphaena: married Antiochus. Cleopatra: m. Lathurus, k. by Tryph. Selene : m. Lathurus; afterwards Antiochus.

Reigns.	Names and Descriptions.	Reigned.	Death.	Wives.	Children.
XI.	SOTER II : Lathurus : Pothinus. With Cleopatra Cocce, his mother.	10 y.	(Deposed.)	1. Cleopatra, his sister. repudiated. 2. Selene : repudiated, and given to Antiochus. 3. A concubine.	Berenice. Auletes. Another son, who reigned in Cyprus, and killed himself. Cleopatra.
XII.	ALEXANDER. Parisactes ; his brother. With Cleopatra Cocce.	17 y. 6 m.	Killed in battle, after killing his mo- ther.	Uncertain.	Alexander II. A daughter : killed with him.
XIII.	SOTER II, again.	8 y.	Natural.		
XIV.	BERENICE, daughter of Soter.	6 m.	Killed by Alexander II.		
XV.	ALEXANDER II. Son of Alexander.	" 8 y. 3 m." [19 d.]	"Dies at Tyre."	Berenice ; whom he killed.	
XVI.	NEUS DIONYSUS : Auletes. Natural son of Lathurus.	" 16 y."		Cleopatra.	Berenice. Cleopatra. Ptolemy : dr. Ptolemy: pois. Arsinoe, left Egypt.
XVII.	BERENICE, daughter of Auletes.	2 y.	Killed by her father.		
XVIII.	AULETES.	2 y.	Natural.		
XIX.	PTOLEMY the elder and Cleopatra, children of Auletes.	3 y.	Drowned after a battle.	Cleopatra his sister.	
XX.	PTOLEMY the younger and Cleopatra.	4 y. 6 m.	Poisoned by his wife.	Cleopatra his sister.	
XXI.	CLEOPATRA, alone.	14 y. 3 m.	Killed herself.	By Julius Caesar. By Antony.	Caesarion. A son. A son. A daughter : carried in triumph by Augustus.

vi. *Approximate dates of the various Reigns; according to Porphyry and to the Medals.*

B. C.	Ptolemy Soter.	B. C.	Philadelphus.	B. C.	Evergetes.	B. C.	Epiphanes.	B. C.	Philometor.
323	1	280	44	236	12	195	11	155	27
322	2	279	45	235	13	194	12	154	28
321	3	278	46	234	14	193	13	153	29
320	4	277	47	233	15	192	14	152	30
319	5	276	48	232	16	191	15	151	31
318	6	275	49	231	17	190	16	150	32
317	7	274	50	230	18	189	17	149	33
316	8	273	51	229	19	188	18	148	34
315	9	272	52	228	20	187	19	147	35
314	10	271	53	227	21	186	20	146	36
313	11	270	54	226	22	185	21		Evergetes. II.
312	12	269	55	225	23	184	22	146	25
311	13	268	56	224	24	183	23	145	26
310	14		{ 57?	223	25	182	24	144	27
309	15	267	{ 19?		Philopator.		Philometor.	143	28
308	16	266	20	222	1	181	1	142	29
307	17	265	21	221	2	180	2	141	30
306	18	264	22	220	3	179	3	140	31
305	19	263	23	219	4	178	4	139	32
304	20	262	24	218	5	177	5	138	33
303	21	261	25	217	6	176	6	137	34
302	22	260	26	216	7	175	7	136	35
301	23	259	27	215	8	174	8	135	36
300	24	258	28	214	9	173	9	134	37
299	25	257	29	213	10	172	10	133	38
298	26	256	30	212	11	171	11	132	39
297	27	255	31	211	12			131	40
296	28	254	32	210	13		Philometor and	130	41
295	29	253	33	209	14		Evergetes II.	129	42
294	30	252	34		Philopator and Epiphanes	170	12—1	128	43
293	31	251	35			169	13—2	127	44
292	32	250	36	208	15	168	14—3	126	45
291	33	249	37	207	16	167	15—4	125	46
290	34	248	38	206	17	166	16—5	124	47
289	35		Evergetes.			165	17—6	123	48
288	36	247	1		Epiphanes			122	49
287	37	246	2	205	1		Philometor.	121	50
286	38	245	3	204	2	164	18	120	51
	Soter and Philadelphus.	244	4	203	3	163	19	179	52
		243	5	202	4	162	20	118	53
285	39	242	6	201	5	161	21	117	54
284	40	241	7	200	6	160	22		Lathurus and Cleopatra.
	Philadelphus.	240	8	199	7	159	23	117	1
283	41	239	9	198	8	158	24	116	2
282	42	238	11	197	9	157	25	115	3
281	43	237	10	196	10	156	26		

B.C. Lathurus and Cleopatra.	B.C. Cleopatra and Alexander.	B.C. Alexander II.	B.C. Auletes.	B.C. Cleopatra and Ptolemy, jun.
114 4	96 22—19	81 1	63 19	48 5--1
113 5	95 23—20	*Auletes.*	62 20	47 6—2
112 6	94 24—21		61 21	46 7—3
111 7	93 25—22	81 1	60 22	45 8—4
110 8	92 26 —23	80 2	59 23	44 9
109 9	91 27—24	79 3	58 24	43 10
108 10	90 28—25	78 4	*Cleopatra and Berenice.*	42 11
Cleopatra and Alexander.	*Alexander.*	77 5		41 12
	89 26	76 6	57 1	40 13
	88 27	75 7	*Berenice.*	39 14
107 11— 8	*Lathurus.*	74 8	56 1	38 15
106 12— 9	88 30	73 9	55 2	37 16—1
105 13—10	87 31	72 10	*Auletes.*	36 17—2
104 14—11	86 32	71 11	54 28	35 18—3
103 15—12	85 33	70 12	53 29	34 19—4
102 16—13	84 34	69 13	*Cleopatra and Ptolemy.*	33 20—5
101 17—14	83 35	68 14	52 1	32 21—6
100 18—15	82 36	67 15	51 2	31 22—7
99 19—16	81 37?	66 16	50 3	
98 20—17	*Berenice.*	65 17	49 4	
97 21--18	81 1	64 18		

OMISSION IN CHAPTER VI.

Page 115. *At the end, add.* To administer
these rites, and to renew these offerings, at least
as often as could be required, was apparently
the duty of the priests, and they were no doubt
amply remunerated for their attentions, by the
families of the deceased, in the form of the
" collections," which are the objects of sale in
Mr. Grey's papyrus. The deed was registered
19 days after its execution.

APPENDIX I.

I. GREEK PAPYRUS OF MR. GREY.

(1) ΑΝΤΙΓΡΑΦον συΝΓΡΑΦΗΣ ΑΙΓΥΠΤΙΑΣ περι νεκΡΩΝ
εν ΘῩν. γενοΜΕΝΗΣ (2) ΚΑΤΑΔ Υ...

(3) ΕΤΟΥΣ Λς αϑυΡ|Κ̄ ΜΕΤΑ ΤΑ ΚΟΙΝΑ ΤΑΔΕ ΛΕΓΕΙ
ΧΟΛΧΥΤΗΣ (4) ΤΩΝ Δουλων ισιδος ΤΗΣ ΜΕΓΑΛΗΣ ΟΝ-
ΝΩΦΡΙΣ ΩΡΟΥ ΜΗΤΡΟΣ (5) ΣΕΝΠΟΗΡις ως ∟ Μ ΕΥ-
ΠΕΤΕΣΙΟΣ ΜΕΓας μελΙΧΡΩΣ ΚΟΙΛΟΦΘΑΛΜΟΣ (6) ΑΝΑ-
ΦΑΛΑΝτος ΩΡΩΙ ΩΡΟΥ ΜΗΤΡΟΣ ΣΕΝΠΟΗΡΙΣ ΗΥΔΟ-
ΚΗσΕ ΑΣΜΕ [νως?] (7) ΤΗΣ ΤΙΜης του ΗΜΙΣΟΥΣ ΤΟΥ
ΤΡΙΤΟΥ της ΛΟΓΕΙΑΣ ΤΩΝ ΚΕΙΜΕΝΩΝ (8) ΝΕΚΡΩΝ εν
ΘΥΝΑΒΟΥΝΟΥΝ ΕΝ τηι ΛΙΒΥΗΙ ΤΟΥ ΠΕΡΙΘΗΒΑΣ (9) ΕΝ
ΤΟΙΣ ΜΕΜΝΟΝΕΙΟΙΣ ΟΜΟΙΩΣ ΚΑΙ ΤΟΥ ΗΜΙΣΟΥΣ ΤΟΥ
ΤΡΙΤΟΥ ΛΕΙΤΟΥΡΓΙΩΝ (10) ΚΑΙ ΤΩΝ ΑΛΛΩΝ ΩΝ ΤΑ Ο-
ΝΟΜΑΤΑ | ΜΟΥϑΗΣ ΣΠΟΤΟΥΤΟΣ ΣΥΝ (11) ΤΕΚΝΟΙΣ ΚΑΙ
πΑΝΤΩΝ ΧΑΠΟΧΡΑΤΗΣ ΝΕΧΘΜΩΝΘΟΥ ΣΥΝ ΤΕΚΝΟΙΣ
(12) ΚΑΙ ΠΑΝΤΩν αΡΣΙΗΣΙΣ ΝΕΧΘΜΩΝΘΟΥ ΟΜΟΙΩΣ
ΠΕΤΕΜΕΣΤΟΥΣ (13) ΝΕΧΘΜωνϑου ΩΣΑΥΤΩΣ ΑΡΣΙΗΣΙΣ
ΖΜΙΝΙΟΣ ΟΜΟΙΩΣ (14) ΟΣΟΡΟΗΡΙΣ ωρου οΜΟΙΩΣ ΣΠΟ-
ΤΟΥΣ ΧΑΠΟΧΩΝΣΙΟΣ ΩΣΑΥΤΩΣ (15) ΖΩΓΛΥΦΟΣ ΑΦ
ΩΝ ΕΠΙΒΑΛΛΕΙ ΑΣΩΤΙ ΩΡΟΥ ΜΗΤΡΟΣ ΣΕΝΠΟΗΡΙΣ (16)
ΤΩΙ ΝΕωτΕΡΟΥ ΣΟΥ ΑΔΕΛΦΩΙ ΤΩΝ ΑΥΤΩΝ ΧΟΛΧΥΤωΝ
ΤΟ ΗΜΙΣΥ (17) ΤΟΥ ΠΡΟΕΙρηΜΕνΟΥ ΤΡΙΤΟΥ ΜΕΡΟΥΣ
ΛΕΙΤΟΥΡΓΙΩΝ ΚΑΙ ΚΑΡΠΕΙΩΝ ΚΑΙ (18) ΤΩΝ ΑΛΛΩν
αΠΕΔΟΤΟ ΑΥΤΩΙ ΕΝ ΤΩΙ λς ‾‾. αϑΥΡ ΕΠΙ ΒΑΣΙΛΕΩΣ (19)
ΑΙΩΝΟΒιΟΥ εις ΠΛΗΡΩΣΙΝ ΤΟΥ ΤΡΙΤΟΥ ΚΑΙ ΤΟΥ ΗΜΙΣΟΥΣ
ΚΑΡΠΕΙΩΝ (20) ΚΑΙ ΤΩΝ ΑΛΛΩν νεΚΡΩΝ ΕΝ ΘΥ. ΠΑ-
ΤΕΥΤΗΜΕΙ ΣΥΝ ΤΕΚΝΟΙΣ ΚΑΙ (21) ΠΑΝΤΩΝ Και ηΜΙΣΟΥΣ

ΚΑΡΠΕΙΩΝ ΕΠΙΒΑΛΛΟΝΤΩΝ ΜΟΙ ΕΝ ΤΟΙΣ (22) ΠΕΤΕΧΩν-
σΙΟΣ ΓΑΛΑΚΤΟΦΟΡΟΥ ΚΑΙ ΤΟΠΟΥ ΑΣΙΗΤΟΣ ΚΑΛΟΥ-
ΜΕΝΟΥ (23) ΦΡΕΚΑΓΗΣ ΣΥΝ ΤΩΝ ΕΝ ΑΥΤωι ΝΕΚΡΩΝ ΑΦ
ΩΝ ΕΠΙΒΑΛΛΕΙ (24) ΤΩΙ ΑΥΤΩΙ ασΩΤΙ ΤΟ ΗΜΙΣΥ ΑΠΕΔΟ-
ΜΗΝ ΑΥΤΩΙ ΣΑ ΕΙΣΙΝ (25) ΚΑΙ ΕΧΩ ΑΥτΩΝ ΠΑΡΑ ΣΟΥ
ΤΗΝ ΤΙΜΗΝ ΚΟΥΘΕΝ ΣΟΙ ΕΓΚΑΛΩ (26) ΠΕΡΙ ΑΥΤΩΝ
αΠΟ ΤΗΣΗΜΕΡΟΝ ΕΑΝ ΔΕ ΤΙΣ ΣΟΙ ΕΠΕΛΘΗΙ (27) ΠΕΡΙ
ΑΥΤΩΝ υΠΟΣΤΗΣΩ ΑΥΤΟΝ ΕΑΝ ΔΕ ΜΗ ΑΠΟΣΤΗΣΩΙ (28)
ΑΠΟΣΤΗΣΩ ΕΠΑΝΑΓΚΟΝ ΕΓΡΑΨΕΝ ΩΡΟΣ ΦΑΒΙΤΟΣ Ο
ΠΑΡΑ ΤΩΝ (29) ΙΕΡΕΙΩΝ του ΑμοΝΡΑΣΟΝΘΗΡ ΚΑΙ ΤΩΝ
ΣΥΝΝΑΩΝ ΘΕΩΝ ΜΟΝΟ(30)ΓΡΑΦΟΣ ΜαρτυΡΕΣ ΕΡΙΕΥΣ
ΦΑΝΡΕΟΥΣ ΠΕΤΕΑΡΤΡΗΣ ΠΑΤΕΥΤΗΜΙΟΣ (31) ΠΕΤΕΑΡ-
ΠΟΧΡΑΤΗΣ ωροΥ ΣΝΑΧΟΜΝΕΥΣ ΠΕΤΕΥΡΙΟΣ ΣΝΑΧΟΜΗΣ
(32) ΨΕΝΧΩΝΣΙΟΣ ΤΟΤΟΗΣ ΦΙΒΙΟΣ ΠΟΡΤΙΣ ΑΠΟΛΛΩΝΙ-
ΟΥ ΖΜΙΝΙΣ (33) ΠΕΤΕΜΕΣΤΟΥΤΟΣ ΠΕΤΕΥΤΗΜΙΣ ΑΡΣΙΗ-
ΣΙΟΣ ΑΜΟΝΟΡΥΤΙΟΣ (34) ΠΑΚΗΜΙΟΣ ΩΡΟΣ ΧΙΜΝΑΡΑΥ-
ΤΟΣ ΑΡΜΗΝΙΣ ΖΘΕΝΑΗΤΙΟΣ (35) ΜΑΗΣΙΣ ΜΙΡΣΙΟΣ ΑΝΤΙ-
ΜΑΧΟΣ ΑΝΤΙΓΕΝΟΥΣ ΠΕΤΟΦΩΙΣ ΦΙΒΙΟΣ (36) ΠΑΝΑΣ
ΠΕΤΟΣΙΡΙΟΣ   ΜΑΡΤΥΡΕΣ ῑϛ
(37) ΑΝΤΙΓΡΑΦΟΝ ΠΤΩΜΑΤΟΣ/ ΕΤΟΥΣ Λϛ ΧΟΙΑΧ ῆ τ ΕΠΙ
ΤΗΝ ΕΝ ΔΙΟΣ⊙ (38) ΤΡΑΠΕΖΑΝ ΕΦ ΗΣ ΛΥΣΙΜΑΧΟΣ Κ ΕΓΚ
ΚΑΤΑ ΔΙΑΓΡΑΦηΝ ΑΣΚΛΗΠΙΑΔΟΥ (19) ΚΑΙ ΖΜΙΝΙΟΣ
ΤΕΛΩΝΩΝ ΕΦ ΗΝ ΥΠΟΓΡ ΠΤΟΛΕΜΑΙΟΣ ΑΝΤΙΓΡ ΩΡΟΣ
ΩΡΟΥ (40) ΧΟΛΧΥΤΗΣ ο π. ΤΩΝ ΛΟΓΕΙΟΜΕΝΩΝ Δι
αυΤΩΝ ΧΑΡΙΝ ΤΩΝ ΚΕΙΜΕΝΩΝ (41) ΝΕΚΡΩΝ ΕΝ· ΘΥΝΑ-
ΒΟΥΝΟΥΝ ΕΝ ΤΟΙΣ ΜΕΜΝΟΝΕΙΟΙΣ ΤΗΣ λιβνΗΣ (42)
Τηϛ ΠΕΡΙ⊖ ΤΑΦΟΙΣ ΑΝΘ ΗΣ ΠΟΙΟΥΝΤΑΙ ΛΕΙΤΟΥΡΓΙΑΣ
Α ΕΩΝΗΣΑΤΟ (43) ΠΑΡΑ ΟΝΝΩΦΡΙΟΣ ΤΟΥ ΩΡΟΥ ΧΑΛ-
ΚοΥ   ΖΓ ῑ̄ Τ,Τ

(44) ΛΥΣΙΜΑΧ . ΥΓῬ

II. PAPYRUS OF ANASTASY AND BÖCKH.

(1) ΒΑΣΙΛΕΥΟΝΤΩΝ ΚΛΕΟΠΑΤΡΑΣ ΚΑΙ ΠΤΟΛΕΜΑΙ·

ΟΥ ΥΙΟΥ ΤΟΥ ΕΠΙΚΑΛΟΥΜΕΝΟΥ ΑΛΕΞΑΝΔΡΟΥ ΘΕΩΝ

ΦΙΛΟΜΗΤΟΡΩΝ ΣΩΤΗΡΩΝ ΕΤΟΥΣ ΙΒ ΤΟΥ ΚΑΙ Θ ΕΦ

ΙΕΡΕΩΣ ΤΟΥ ΟΝΤΟΣ (2)ΕΝ ΑΛΕΧΑΝΔΡΕΙΑΙ ΑΛΕΞΑΝ ΔΡΟΥ

ΚΑΙ ΘΕΩΝ ΣΩΤΗΡΩΝ ΚΑΙ ΘΕΩΝ ΑΔΕΛΦΩΝ ΚΑΙ ΘΕΩΝ

ΕΥΕΡΓΕΤΩΝ ΚΑΙ ΘΕΩΝ ΦΙΛΟΠΑΤΟΡΩΝ ΚΑΙ ΘΕΩΝ ΕΠΙ-

ΦΑΝΩΝ ΚΑΙ ΘΕΟΥ (3) ΦΙΛΟΜΗΤΟΡΟΣ ΚΑΙ ΘΕΟΥ ΕΥΠΑ-

ΤΟΡΟΣ ΚΑΙ ΘΕΩΝ ΕΥΕΡΓΕΤΩΝ ΑΘΛΟΦΟΡΟΥ ΒΕΡΕΝΙΚΗΣ

ΕΥΕΡΓΕΤΙΔΟΣ ΚΑΝΗΦΟΡΟΥ ΑΡΣΙΝΟΗΣ ΦΙΛΑΔΕΛΦΟΥ

ΚΑΙ [ΙΕΡΕΙ]ΑΣ ΑΡΣΙΝΟΗΣ (4) ΕΥΠΑΤΟΡΟΣ ΤΩΝ ΟΝΤΩΝ

ΕΝ ΑΛΕΞΑΝΔΡΕΙΑΙ ΕΝ ΔΕ ΠΤΟΛΕΜΑΙΔΙ ΤΗΣ ΘΗΒΑΙΔΟΣ

ΕΦ ΙΕΡΕΩΝ ΠΤΟΛΕΜΑΙΟΥ ΤΟΥ ΜΕΝ ΣΩΤΗΡΟΣ ΤΩΝ ΟΝ-

ΤΩΝ ΚΑΙ ΟΥΣΩΝ (5) ΕΝ ΠΤΟΛΕΜΑΙΔΙ ΜΗΝΟΣ ΤΥΒΙ Κ̅Θ̅

ΕΠ ΑΠΟΛΛΩΝΙΟΥ ΤΟΥ ΠΡΟΣ ΤΗΙ ΑΓΟΡΑΝΟΜΙΑΙ ΤΩΝ Μ̅Ε̅

ΚΑΙ ΤΗΣ ΚΑΤΩ ΤΟΠΑΡΧΙΑΣ ΤΟΥ ΠΑΘΥΡΙΤΟΥ

(6) ΛΠΕΔΟΤΟ ΠΑΜΩΝΘΗΣ ΩΣ ∟ ΜΕ ΜΕΣΟΣ ΜΕΛΑΝΧΡΩΣ

ΚΑΛΟΣ ΤΟ ΣΩΜΑ ΦΑΛΑΚΡΟΣ ΣΤΡΟΓΓΥΛΟΠΡΟΣΩΠΟΣ

ΕΥΘΥΡΙΝ ΚΑΙ ΣΝΑΧΟΜΝΕΥΣ ΩΣ ∟ Κ ΜΕΣΟΣ ΜΕΛΙΧΡΩΣ

(7)ΚΑΙ ΟΥΤΟΣ ΣΤΡΟΓΓΥΛΟΠΡΟΣΩΠΟΣ ΕΥΘΥΡΙΝ ΚΑΙ ΣΕΜ-

ΜΟΥΘΙΣ ΠΕΡΣΙΝΗΙ ΩΣ ∟ ΚΒ ΜΕΣΗΙ ΜΕΛΙΧΡΩΣ ΣΤΡΟΓΓΥ-

ΛΟΠΡΟΣΩΠΟΣ ΕΝΣΙΜΟΣ ΗΣΥΧΗ ΚΑΙ ΤΑΘΛΥΤ (8) ΠΕΡ-

ΣΙΝΗΙ ΩΣ ∟ Λ ΜΕΣΗΙ ΜΕΛΙΧΡΩΣ ΣΤΡΟΓΓΥΛΟΠΡΟΣΩΠΟΣ

ΕΥΘΥΡΙΝ ΜΕΤΑ ΚΥΡΙΟΥ ΤΟΥ ΕΑΥΤΩΝ ΠΑΜΩΝΘΟΥ ΤΟΥ

ΣΥΝΑΠΟΔΟΜΕΝΟΥ ΟΙ ΤΕΣΣΑΡΕΣ (9) ΤΩΝ ΠΕΤΕΨΑΙΤΟΣ

ΤΩΝ ΕΚ ΤΩΝ ΜΕΜΝΟΝΕΙΩΝ ΣΚΥΤΕΩΝ ΑΠΟ ΤΟΥ ΥΠΑΡ-

ΧΟΝΤΟΣ ΑΥΤΟΙΣ ΕΝ ΤΩΙ ΑΠΟ ΝΟΤΟΥ ΜΕΡΕΙ ΜΕΜΝΟ-
ΝΕΩΝ ΠΛΑΚΟ"Υ"Σ (10) ΨΙΛΟΥ ΤΟΠΟΥ ΠΗΧΕΙΣ ΕΝ ΤΕΤΑΡ-
ΤΟΝ Η ΓΕΙΤΟΝΕΣ ΝΟΤΟΥ ΡΥΜΗ ΒΑΣΙΛΙΚΗ ΒΟΡΡΑ ΚΑΙ
ΑΠΗΛΙΩΤΟΥ ΠΑΜΩΝΘΟΥ ΚΑΙ ΒΟΚΟΝΣΙΗΜΙΟΣ ΑΔΕΛΦΟΣ
(11) ΚΑΙ ΚΟΙΝΟΣ ΠΟΛΕΩΣ [or ΤΟΙΧΟΣ]   ΛΙΒΟΣ ΟΙΚΙΑ
ΤΑΓΗΤΟΣ ΤΟΥ ΧΑΛΟΜΗ ΡΕΟΥΣΗΣ ΑΝΑ ΜΕΣΟΝ ΔῚ
ΦΕρΟΥΣΗΣ ΑΠΟ ΤΟΥ Π͞Ο ΓΕΙΤΟΝΕΣ ΠΑΝΤΟΘΕΝ ΕΠΡΙΑ-
ΤΟ ΝΕΧΟΥΤΗΣ ΜΙΚΡΟΣ (12) ΑΣΩΤΟΣ ΩΣ ∟ Μ ΜΕΣΟΣ
ΜΕΛΙΧΡΩΣ ΤΕΡΠΝΟΣ ΜΑΚΡΟΠΡΟΣΩΠΟΣ ΕΥΘΥΡΙΝ ΟΥΑΗ
ΜΕΤΩΠΩΙ ΜΕΣΩΙ ΧΑΛΚΟΥ ΝΟΜΙΣΜΑΤΟΣ Χ͞Α ΠΡΟΠΩ-
ΛΗΤΑΙ ΚΑΙ (13) ΒΕΒΑΙΩΤΑΙ ΤΩΝ ΚΑΤΑ ΤΗΝ ΩΝΗΝ ΤΑΥ-
ΤΗΝ ΟΙ ΑΠΟΔΟΜΕΝΟΙ ΕΝΕΔΕΞ͢ΑΤΟ ΝΕΧΟΥΤΗΣ Ο
ΠΡΙΑΜΕΝΟΣ

ΑΠΟΛ . Κ . Α͞γρ .

L. 9. ΠΛΑΚΟΥΣ for ΠΛΑΚΟΣ. L. 10. ΑΔΕΛΦΟΣ seems
inserted parenthetically. L. 11. ΔΙ for ΔΙΩΡΥΓΟΣ.
L. 13. Possibly Ο ΕΔΕΞ͢ΑΤΟ, but not ΟΝ.L. 14. The signature
somewhat resembles the Κ' ΕΓΚν, which occurs in almost all
the registers; but from the interpretation of that contraction,
afforded by the Parisian manuscript, it would be unapplicable
here; and these characters may probably be part of κατ'
ἀγοράν. The term λόγεια, or λογία, of the former manuscript,
was afterwards applied to the collections made for the poor,
in the Christian Churches.

III. VARIOUS REGISTRIES COMPARED.

1. **GREY. A.**   ΕΤΟΥΣ ΚΗ ΜΕΣΟΡΗ ΚΗ̄
2. **B.**   ΕΤΟΥΣ ΚΘ ΦΑΜ^{ε} Θ̄
3. **C.**   ΕΤΟΥΣ ΛΕ ΦΑΡΜΟ^{ν} Κ̄
4. **PARIS. ENCH.**   ΕΤΟΥΣ Λϛ ΧΟΙΑΧ Θ̄
5. **GREY ANT.**   ΕΤΟΥΣ Λϛ ΧΟΙΑΧ Θ̄
6. **ANASTASY.**   ΕΤΟΥΣ ΙΒ ΤΟΥ ΚΑΙ Θ ΦΑΡΜΟΥΘΙ Κ̄

1. ΓΕΓ̄   ΕΠΙ ΤΗΝ   ΕΝ ΕΡΜΩ2ΕΙ
2. ΓΕΓ̄   ΕΠΙ ΤΗΝ   ΕΝ ΕΡΜ^{ω}
3. ΤΕΤ̄   ΕΠΙ ΤΗΝ   ΕΝ ΔΙΟΣ⊙ ΤΗΙ Μ^{ε}
4. ΤΕΤΑΚΤΑΙ ΕΠΙ ΤΗΝ   ΕΝ ΔΙΟΣΠΟΛΕΙ ΤΗΙ ΜΕΓΑΛΗΙ
5. Τ   ΕΠΙ ΤΗΝ   ΕΝ ΔΙΟΣ⊙
6. ...   ΕΠΙ ΤΗΝ   ΕΝ ΕΡ2

1. ΤΡ̄   ΕΦ ΗΣ ΔΙΌ   Κ́   ΕΓΚ̄^{υ}
2. ΤΡ̄   ΕΦ ΗΣ ΔΙΟΝ̄   Κ́   ΕΓΚ̄^{υ}
3. ΤΡ̄   ΕΦ ΗΣ ΛΥΣΙΜ
4. ΤΡΑΠΕΖΑΝ ΕΦ ΗΣ ΛΥΣΙΜΑΧΟΣ ΕΙΚΟΣΤΗΣ ΕΓΚΥΚΛΙΟΥ
5. ΤΡΑΠΕΖΑΝ ΕΦ ΗΣ ΛΥΣΙΜΑΧΟΣ Κ   ΕΓΚ̄^{υ}
6. ΤΡ̄   ΕΦ ΗΣ ΔΙΟΝ̄^{υ} Κ̄   ΕΓΚ̄^{υ}

1. ΚΑΤΑ ΤΗΝ ΠΑΡ ΑΣΚΛ^Η
2. ΚΑΤΑ ΤΗΝ ΠΑΡ ΑΣΚΛ̄ ΚΑΙ ΚΡΑΤΟΥ
3. ΚΑΤΑ ΤΗΝ ΠΑΡΑ ΣΑΡΑΠΙΩΝΟΣ ΚΑΙ ΤΩΝ ΜΕΤΟΧΩΝ
4. ΚΑΤΑ ΔΙΑΓΡΑΦΗΝ ΑΣΚΛΗΠΙΑΔΟΥ ΚΑΙ ΖΜΙΝΙΟΣ
5. ΚΑΤΑ ΔΙΑΓΡΑΦηΝ ΑΣΚΛΗΠΙΑΔΟΥ ΚΑΙ ΖΜΙΝΙΟΣ
6. ΚΑΤΑ ΔΙΑΓΡ̄ $\mu\epsilon\tau o\chi^{\omega}$

1. ΤΟΥ ΠΡΟΣ ΤΗΙ ΩΝΗΙ ΔΙΑΓΡ̄ ΥΦ ΗΝ ΥΠΟΓΡ ΠΤΟΛ^ε
2. ΤΩΝ ΠΡΟΣ ΤΗΙ ΩΝΗ ΔΙΑΓΡ̄ ΥΦ ΗΝ ΥΠΟΓΡ̄ ΠΤΟΛΕΜΑΙΟΣ
3. ΤΩΝ ΠΡΟΣ ΤΗΙ ΩΝΗΙ ΔΙΑΓΡ̄ ΥΦ ΗΝ ΥΠΟΓΡ ΕΡΜΟΦΙΛΟΣ
4. ΤΕΛΩΝΩΝ ΥΦ ΗΝ ΥΠΟΓΡ̄ ΠΤΟΛΕΜΑΙΟΣ
5. ΤΕΛΩΝΩΝ ΥΦ ΗΝ ΥΠΟΓΡ̄ ΠΤΟΛΕΜΑΙΟΣ
6. ΤΕ^λ ΥΦ ΗΝ ΥΠΟΓΡ ΗΡΚΛΕΙΔΗΣ

1. ΑΝΤΙΓΡ̄ ΩΝΗΣ ΤΕΕΦΒΙΣ ΑΜΕΝ^ω
2. Ο ΑΝΤΙΓΡ̄ ΑΣΥΣ ΩΡΟΥ ΩΝΗΣ
3. ΚΑΙ ΣΑΡ̄ ΟΙ ΑΝΤΙΓΡ̄ ΩΝΗΣ ΠΕΧΥΤΗΣ ΑΡΣΙΗΣΙΟΣ
4. Ο ΑΝΤΙΓΡ̄ $\alpha\sigma\omega$Σ ΩΡΟΥ ΧΟΛΧΥΤΟΥ
5. ΑΝΤΙΓΡ̄ ΩΡΟΣ ΩΡΟΥ ΧοΛΧΥΤΗΣ
6. Ο ΑΝΤΙΓΡ̄ ΤΗ̂ ΩΝΗΣ ΝΕΧΟΥΤΗΣ ΜΙΚΡΟΣ ΑΣΩΤΟΣ

1. ΤΧΧ | ΑΠΟ Π̇² ⊥ Ẑ ΑΠΟ Ν̇ ΤΟΥ ΟΛΟΥ ΨΙΛΟΥ Τ̇
2. ΨΙΛΟΥ Τ̇ Β̂__
3. Δ′ ΜΕΡΟΥΣ ΨΙΛΟΥ Τ̇ Γ̂ ∠
4. ΕΝ Η: ΤΩΝ ΛΟΓΕΙΟΜΕΝΩΝ ΔΙ ΑΥΤΩΝ ΧΑΡΙΝ ΤΩΝ
5. ιΝ η. ΤΩΝ ΛΟΓΕΙΟΜΕΝΩΝ ΔΙ ΑΥΤΩΝ ΧΑΡΙΝ ΤΩΝ
6. ΨΙΛΟΝ ΤΟΠΟΝ Η̄ ΕΝ ΤΕΤΑΡΤον

1. ΤΟΥ ΟΝΤΟΣ ΑΠΟ ΝΟΤΟΥ ΔΙΟΣ⊙ ΤΗΣ Μ^ε

2. ΤΟΥ ΟΝΤΟΣ ΑΠΟ Ν̊ ΔΙΟΣ⊙ ΤΗΣ Μ^ε

3. ΕΝ ΤΩΙ ΑΠΟ Ν̊ Μ^ε ΔΙΟΣ⊙ ΤΗΣ Μ⁻ ΑΠΟ ΛΙΒΟΣ

4. ΚΕΙΜΕΝΩΝ ΝΕΚΡΩΝ ΕΝ ΟΙΣ ΕΧΟΥΣΙΝ ΕΝ ΤΟΙΣ

5. ΚΕΙΜΕΝΩΝ ΝΕΚΡΩΝ ΕΝ ΘΥΝΑΒΟΥΝΟΥΝ ΕΝ ΤΟΙΣ

6. ΕΝ ΤΩΙ ΑΠΟ ΝΟΤΟΥ ΜΕΡΕΙ ΜΕΜΝΟΝΕΩΝ

3. ΤΟΥ ωΡ° ΤΟΥ ΗΡ ΤΟΥ ΑΓΟΝΤΟΣ ΕΠΙ ΠΟΤ̄

4. ΜΕΜΝΟΝΕΙΟΙΣ ΤΗΣ ΛΙΒΥΗΣ ΤΟΥ ΠΕΡΙΘΗΒαΣ ΤΑΦΟΙΣ

5. ΜΕΜΝΟΝΕΙΟΙΣ ΤΗΣ ΛΙβνΗΣ Τον ΠΕΡῙΘ ΤΑΦΟΙΣ

1. ΩΝ ΑΙ ΓΕΙΤΝΙΑΙ ΔΕΔ ΔΙΑ ΤΗΣ ΠΡΟΚ^ε ΣΥΝΓΡ

2. ΟΥ ΑΙ ΓΕΙΤΝΙΑΙ ΔΕΔ ΔΙΑ ΤΗΣ ΠΡ̊ ΣΥΝΓΡ̄

3. ΟΥ ΑΙ ΓΕΙΤΝΙΑΙ ΔΕΔ ΔΙΑ ΤΗΣ ΠΡΟΚΕΙΜΕ ΣΥΝΓΡ̄

4. ΑΝΘ ΗΣ ΠΟΙΕΙΤΑΙ ΛΕΙΤΟΥΡΓΙΑΣ

5. ΑΝΘ ΗΣ ΠΟΙΟΥΝΤΑΙ ΛΕΙΤΟΥΡΓΙΑΣ

1. ΟΝ ΗΓΟ̄Ρ ΠΑΡ ΑΛΗΚΙΟΣ ΚΑΙ

2. Ον ΗΓ̄ ΠΑΡ ΑΛΗΚΙΟΣ ΤΟΥ ΕΡΙΕΩΣ ΚΑΙ

3. ΟΝ ΗΓΟΡΑΣΕΝ ΠΑΡ ΑΜΜΩΝΙΟΥ ΤΟΥ ΠΥΡΡΙΟΥ ΚΑΙ

4. Α ΕΩΝ^η ΠΑΡ ΟΝΝΩΦΡΙΟΣ ΤΟΥ ΩΡΟΥ

5. Α ΕΩΝΗΣΑΤΟ ΠΑΡΑ ΟΝΝΩΦΡΙΟΣ ΤΟΥ ΩΡΟΥ

6. ΟΝ ΕΩΝΗΘΗ ΠΑΡ̄ ΠΑΜΩΝΘΗΣΤΟΥ ΚΑΙ

1. ΛΟΥΒΑΙΤΟΣ ΚΑΙ ΤΒΑΙΑΙΤΟΣ ΤΩΝ ΕΡΙΕΩΣ ΚΑΙ

2. ΛΟΥΒΑΙΤΟΣ ΚΑΙ ΤΒΑΙΑΙΤΟΣ ΤΩΝ ΕΡΙΕΩΣ ΚΑΙ

3. ΨΕΝΑΜΟΥΝΙΟΣ ΤΟΥ ΠΥΡΡΙΟΥ

6. ΣΝΑΧΟΜΝΕΩΣ ΤΩΝ ΠΕΤΕΨΑΙΤΟΣ ΣΥΝ ΤΑΙΣ ΑΔΕΛΦΑΙΣ

1. ΣΕΝΕΡΙΕΥΤΟΣ ΤΗΣ ΠΕΤΕΝΕΦΩΤΟΥ ΚΑΙ ΕΡΙΕΩΣ ΤΟΥ
2. ΣΕΝΕΡΙΕΩΣ   ΤΗΣ ΠΕΤΕΝΕΦΩΤΟΥ ΚΑΙ ΕΡΙΕΩΣ ΤΟΥ

1. ΑΜΕΝΩΘΟΥ ΚΑΙ ΣΕΝΟΣΟΡΦΙΒΙΟΣ ΤΗΣ ΑΜΕΝΩΘΟΥ
2. ΑΜΕΝΩΘΟΥ ΚΑΙ ΣΕΝΟΣΟΡΦΙΒΙΟΣ ΤΗΣ ΑΜΕΝΩΘΟΥ

1. ΚΑΙ ΣΠΟΙΤΟΣ ΤΟΥ ΚΑΙ ΕΡΙΕΩΣ ΤΟΥ ΑΜΕΝΩΘΟΥ
2. ΚΑΙ·ΣΠΟΙΤΟΣ   ΚΑΙ ΕΡΙΕΩΣ ΤΟΥ ΑΜΕΝΩΘΟΥ

1. ΕΝ ΤΩΙ ΚΗ ΠΑΧΩΝ|$\overline{\text{Κ}}$
4. ΕΝΤΩΙ Λς L ΑΘΥΡ Κης

1.	$\overline{\text{Χ}}\overline{\text{Χ}}$	τελος
2.	$\overline{\chi}\ \overline{\chi}\ a\ \delta$	τελος
3.	ΧΑλκ ΓιΒ	$\overset{c}{\text{Τ}}$
4. ΣΥΙΝΕΤΡΑΠΗΣΘΗΙ	ΧΑΛΚΟΥ ¿ΧΣ? ΤΕΛΟΣ	
5.	ΧΑΛΚΟΥ ΖΓ	$\overline{\text{Τ}}$
6.	$\overline{\text{Χ}}$	Ζ α

1. της δ	Ρ | Ρ ΔΙΟΝ	$\overline{\text{ΥΡ}}$
2. ου ακ	Φ ΔΙΟΝ$^{\nu}$	ΥΡ
3. ου $\overset{\wedge}{\Lambda}$	R / R ΛΥΣΙΜΑΧ	$\overline{\text{ΥΓΡ}}$
4. ΕΝΑΚοιΟΥΣ	| Ι ΛΥΣΙΜΑΧΟΣ	$\overset{\varepsilon}{\text{Υγϱ}}$
5.	Τ | Τ ΛΥΣΙΜΑΧ	$\overline{\text{ΥΓΡ}}$
6. $\overset{\wedge}{\eta}$ = χ	$\underset{\iota}{\Delta}$	$\overline{\text{ΥΓΡ}}$

APPENDIX II.

From the Article EGYPT.

1. GOD; *powerful*

2. GOD; *judge*

3. GODDESS

4. GODS

5. AGATHODAEMON

6. PHTHAH

7. AMMON

8. PHRE

9. RHEA

10. IOH

11. THOTH

12. OSIRIS

13. ARUERIS

14. Isis

15. Nephthe

16. Buto

17. Horus

20. Apis

22. Hyperion

23. Cteristes [or Cerberus]

24. Tetrarcha

25. Anubis

26. Macedo

27. Hieracion

28. Cerexochus

30. Platypterus

38. Memnon

50. Psammis

52. Amasis

57. Soteres

72. Ramuneus

80. Egypt

81. Memphis

83. Greek.

84. Country

85. Land

87. Temple

88. Shrine

91 Column

92. Diadem

100. Tear

101. Image

102. Statue

103. LETTERS

108. LIFE

109. ETERNITY

110. IMMORTAL

111. JOY

112. POWER

113. STABILITY

114. ESTABLISHED

116. MIGHTY

117. VICTORY

118. FORTUNE

119. SPLENDOUR

120 BEARING

121. ILLUSTRIOUS

122. HONOUR

123 RESPECTABLE { " אֵי? "   (hieroglyphics)

             " דְּשׁוּא? "   (hieroglyph)

125. RITE   (hieroglyphics)

126. WORSHIP   (hieroglyph)

127. FATHER   (hieroglyph)

129. SON   (hieroglyph)

133. CHILD   (hieroglyph)

(128.) [WIFE]   (hieroglyphics)

[BROTHER; SISTER   (hieroglyphics)]

134. DIRECTOR   (hieroglyph)

135. STEERSMAN   (hieroglyphics)

137. KING   (hieroglyphics)

138. CONDITION   (hieroglyph)

139. KINGDOM   (hieroglyphics)

140. LIBATION   (hieroglyphics)

142 PRIEST

143. PRIESTHOOD

145. ASSEMBLY

146. SACRED

147. CONSECRATED

148. GIVE

149. OFFER

151. LAWFUL

152. GOOD

153. BESTOWING

154. MUNIFICENT

155. UPPER; LOWER

156. OTHERS

160. ENLIGHTENING

162. LOVING

164. SET UP

165. PREPARE

166. IN ORDER THAT

167. WHEREVER

168. AND
169. ALSO, WITH

170. MOREOVER

171. LIKEWISE

172 IN

173. UPON, AT

174. OVER, ON

175. FOR

176. BY THE

177. OF, TO

178. DAY

179. MONTH

180. YEAR

181. THOYTH

182. MECHIR

183. MESORE

184. FIRST DAY

185. THIRTIETH

186. ONE

187. FIRST

188. TWO

192. THRICE

197. TEN

200. FORTY TWO

201. A HUNDRED

202. A THOUSAND

Howlett and Brimmer, Printers,
10, Frith Street, Soho.